# *Grace Upon Grace*

*God's Faithfulness Abounds*

*To my dear wife Jessica; my helpmate*
*and the answer to so many prayers.*

*And to our precious daughter Selah,*
*may we always remember to pause and reflect*
*on God's Word.*

*Many thanks to all who encouraged me*
*to capture these testimonies*
*to share with others.*

# Contents

Preface

1. The Beginning 1

2. Learning to Love 7

3. Trusting God for Fruit 19

4. Learning to Hear God's Voice 27

5. Divine Appointments 33

6. Walking Through Open Doors 41

7. Releasing Our Agenda for God's Agenda 61

8. The Power of Prayer 75

9. The Power of Intercessory Prayer 91

10. Experiencing Blessings Through Obedience 105

11. God is Sovereign 113

12. Believe and Follow 129

13. His Grace is Sufficient 139

14. Helping Others 147

Epilogue

# *Preface*

The intent of this book is to point you toward God and into a deeper understanding of His faithfulness. The Spirit-filled Christian life is one of glorifying God, learning more of His character, seeking His presence, and following Him wherever He leads. Herein is a personal account of how He has taken me on an incredible journey of catching glimpses of His amazing grace. The depths of the riches of His love, grace, and mercy are truly unparalleled. I relate the intent of this book with the beginning of Psalm 105:

> "Oh give thanks to the Lord; call upon his name;
>     make known his deeds among the peoples!
> [2] Sing to him, sing praises to him;
>     tell of all his wondrous works!
> [3] Glory in his holy name;
>     let the hearts of those who seek the Lord rejoice!
> [4] Seek the Lord and his strength;
>     seek his presence continually!"

As I hope you will see through the experiences I have attempted to capture in this book, God is not distant. He is right here with us, completely mindful of our personal experiences as we endeavor to simply believe and follow Him.

I quickly learned that to make sure I am following Him, I needed to discern His voice. As He speaks, my role is simply to respond by faith in obedience, trusting Him through the journey, as well as the outcome.

Even at this very moment, I am praying for Him to guide my thoughts and hands as I write this in service to Him. I pray this book is a blessing to you and that somehow you might be drawn closer to God, not because of my efforts, but by His grace as He speaks to you.

*May God richly bless you as you seek more of Him.*

# Chapter 1

## *The Beginning*

The only way to have a true relationship with God is to receive and confess Jesus Christ as your very own personal Lord and Savior. At that moment, the living God takes residence within you and you can become a saved child of God. This was a truth I learned through the Word of God and personal experience.

It initially happened to me when I was quite young. After hearing the Gospel message that we are all born with sin in our lives and that Jesus is the way for our forgiveness, I responded to this Good News and was ready to receive Him as my Savior. I clearly remember the moment of that simple prayer.

I grew up in a multicultural household in Charlotte, North Carolina. My father immigrated to the United States from Iran and my mother is a native of North Carolina. I had not traveled very much in the years I was in school, and the city I lived in grew significantly in population during that time.

Over the years, that initial seed of faith grew and then waned. By the time I was in college, I had drifted away and wanted mostly to fulfill worldly desires. I simply wanted to get the most material possessions, to feel the best, and to exert the least amount of energy as possible to fulfill these goals.

This eventually led me to an emptiness that was never satisfied. The more possessions I obtained, and the better I thought I felt, the less valuable more of the same seemed to be. I began to wonder if there was more to life than running on this never-ending cycle of temporary and deceiving self-fulfillment.

Through an array of difficult experiences that followed, I finally found myself utterly lost and depressed. This led me through a period of addiction, anxiety, and depression. I eventually found myself at a point of complete brokenness.

It was at that time when I found myself at the end of my rope. I was searching for real answers to serious life questions. I wanted real solutions to my emptiness inside. There was such an inward void and pain that led to despair and a sense of hopelessness. I was exhausted and hurting to a point of giving up on life, and ultimately not caring what would happen to me any longer.

I finally got to the point of boldness, asking God directly to reveal Himself to me. I said something like, "God, if you are real, I need you to reveal yourself to me and give me a plan and a purpose for my life."

*He did.*

Approximately three weeks later I had an amazing encounter with the True and Living God. I know this can sound surreal, but it is the truth. It happened just prior to 4 o'clock in the morning. I was awoken from a vivid dream. God began to speak to me, and He gave me clear and specific instructions for work that He wanted me to do during that season of my life.

I could not believe it and began to doubt right away. As I pondered what had just happened, I began to sense God's presence throughout my entire body. I had never experienced anything like it. He confirmed through His presence what He had just said.

I fell on the floor, and for the first time, as I felt so dirty and unworthy, I offered every single ounce of myself to Him. At that moment of surrender, it felt as if the Lord was embracing me as the prodigal son returning home and receiving complete forgiveness. I felt the Holy Spirit shower over me, and for the first time, I knew that I was completely in God's hands—and that everything was going to be ok.

If you are unfamiliar with the presence of God, you may have a hard time understanding this point. The Good News is God can and will reveal Himself to us through the power of the Gospel. Jesus took the full punishment of our sins. He loves us that much.

I knew from that moment, without a doubt, that God is real, heaven is real, and that this life is temporary and passing by fast. I did not want to waste any more time. That experience changed the whole direction of my life.

When I had this encounter with God and truly understood that Jesus Christ was His Son, the Savior of the world, I wanted to tell everybody. I thought to myself, "They might think I'm crazy, but I've got to tell them the truth. I've got to tell people about Jesus and let them know God's Word is real!"

Even though I had so much zeal, God began to humble me. Through drawing closer to Him, He showed me that my job was to follow Him. If I would simply believe Him and follow where He leads, He would be glorified in my life and I could bear eternal fruit. It was up to God to open the doors for me to share Christ with others. My job was to be obedient as I remained sensitive to His will. The beauty of this learning process is how patient God was with me.

Right away, God gave me a unique assignment. He prompted me to visit a different church every Sunday for an entire year. Therefore, every Sunday I visited a different church and brought along a journal to take notes. Some Sundays I woke up and did not know where to visit, so I prayed, and God revealed to me exactly where to go each time. I documented the message that was preached and wrote about the unique nature of each experience. I visited Christian churches of every denomination, with great variety of size and demographics among the congregations.

During my visits, I noted the style of worship, as well as the atmosphere of the church environment including the details of the meeting space and the building. This went on for 57 weeks in a row, until God placed me in the church where He wanted me to become a member. Throughout that experience, God was revealing to me that details such as the worship style or the sign on the outside of the building were insignificant compared to the heart of the people inside. It was not so much about the rituals of the church services, but much more so about the relationships people had with Him. He was showing me that all that really mattered was Christ in us, the hope of glory.

As you will see, I began to learn by experience, and throughout this book I will share many instances of how God has dealt with me as I have endeavored to follow Him. I hope to share these experiences as accurately as possible through humility. Despite my weaknesses, fears, and doubts, God has allowed me to follow Him to many places and to trust Him for the results. I pray you will be encouraged and refreshed as I try to share with great and authentic detail my personal experiences of God's sovereignty and His might amid these many circumstances.

Know that I have already prayed for you as you read through this book. Please take a moment and pause now to pray that God would show you what He wants you to see as you read further. No matter where you are on your faith journey, you can pray a simple prayer that might be something like:

*"God, please reveal to me what You want me to see."*

# Chapter 2

## Learning to Love

As I began to walk with God daily, seeking more of His presence and learning more of His character, He began to teach me to love others. In the past, I had always tried to outsmart others, and, in effect, control my environment. God started to humble me to see others as He does: beautiful works of His creation, made in His image.

He began to break me of my pride, and I began to see myself as equal with others, and then eventually more as a servant of God in others' lives. God began to show me His patience and grace in their lives, and He wanted me to be patient and extend them grace, as well. We read about having speech filled with grace in Colossians 4:6:

> "Let your speech always be gracious, seasoned with salt, so that you may know how you ought to answer each person."

Even with good intentions of extending grace and being patient, sometimes conversations are not easy. People are not always so eager and willing to hear the Good News. Maybe they have been hurt badly, or just need to vent. Sometimes people are even confrontational. No matter the outcome, or where a person happens to be at a point in time, I believe our job is to simply love them right where they are, trusting God for the fruit.

One such occasion happened while I was on a plane traveling from Charlotte, North Carolina to Nashville, Tennessee. As the plane was getting ready to depart the terminal, all seats were full except one open spot on the whole plane. This open spot happened to be a middle seat next to me. I sat at a window seat, and another person was sitting in the aisle seat.

As the flight attendant began the announcements, a last-minute passenger scrambled quickly onto the plane. It was a young lady and she struggled to cram her carry-on luggage into a small space in an overhead bin. She then made her way over to the last seat, next to me. As I had learned to do many times over the years, I moved the seat belts to the sides of the seat so she could sit down. She expressed appreciation and hurriedly took her seat.

The plane began preparations for taxiing to the runway when the young lady started a conversation with me. I shared with her that I was originally from Charlotte but now lived in Nashville. I told her I travelled a lot and she asked why. I responded that I traveled extensively with mission work to help share the Gospel.

At that point, she began to share with me all the reasons she did not like Christians. To my surprise, she began to vent quite extensively. I found out the extent of her pain centered on a Christian aunt, who somehow gave her a hard time. The more she vented, the more awkward the conversation became. It felt as if she was directing all her negative energy toward Christians right onto me.

While she was talking, something quite unusual, yet incredible, happened. The Lord began to give me a glimpse of His amazing love for this young woman. As I began to feel God's love for her, she literally began to glow! God was preparing me to be His vessel at that moment. After she was finished venting, I began to share with her my testimony. I shared with her that years ago I was in so much pain, felt hopeless and lost, and how I eventually called out to the Lord. I then shared how He answered my prayer and saved me with His amazing grace. After I shared, she looked at me and said something I could have never imagined.

She told me that she was suicidal and shared that she had already tried to commit suicide three times. She shared that she was not from the east coast, and the only reason she was traveling was that it was a last-minute effort by her family to get her into a facility to

9

receive the help she needed. Let us take a pause here for a moment.

*A young woman who I never met before just told me on a crowded airplane that she was suicidal.*

I would not have known exactly how to respond, but God knew what she needed to hear. In that very moment, Scripture began to well up inside of me. I shared with her a passage from Jeremiah 29:11, that God had a plan for her life, not to harm her but to give her hope and a future. Her eyes dropped and she began to stare at the back of the passenger seat in front of me. I continued pouring out words of truth and hope, sharing the love of God in Christ for her. I cannot recall everything I said, but God gave me free-flowing words for the next ten minutes. I shared with her that giving her life to the Lord was the best thing she could ever do.

Before the plane made its final descent into Nashville, we were bowing our heads, praying for her life to be dedicated to the Lord. I pulled out a Bible to give her and wrote an inscription on the inside, "Buckle up, enjoy the ride," which hinted to the initial contact we had when I helped clear her seat of the seat belts. She had an appearance of hope as she departed the plane. Praise God for His love that can flow through willing vessels, even amid a negative circumstance. What a divine appointment!

As I learned to love others with a sincere desire to share the Good News, I became amazed at the simplicity of sharing the Gospel. I am so glad God made it easy to share and communicate. I cannot help but wonder if somehow, we seem to make a way of overcomplicating it. It is as easy as the following simple points:

1. God loves everyone
2. Everyone is a sinner
3. God made a remedy for sin
4. Anyone can be saved

*Could it really be that easy? How can we be confident that these simple points are true?*

We can be confident because each one is backed by Scripture:

God's love for everyone:

John 3:16

"For God so loved the world, that he gave his only Son, that whoever believes in him should not perish but have eternal life."

Romans 5:8

"But God shows his love for us in that while we were still sinners, Christ died for us."

Everyone is a sinner:

Romans 3:23

"For all have sinned and fall short of the glory of God."

Romans 3:10

"As it is written: 'None is righteous, no, not one.'"

11

## God made a remedy for sin:

Romans 6:23

"For the wages of sin is death, but the free gift of God is eternal life in Christ Jesus our Lord."

John 1:12

"But to all who did receive him, who believed in his name, he gave the right to become children of God."

1 Corinthians 15:3-4

"For I delivered to you as of first importance what I also received: that Christ died for our sins in accordance with the Scriptures, that he was buried, that he was raised on the third day in accordance with the Scriptures."

Ephesians 2:8

"For by grace you have been saved through faith. And this is not of your own doing; it is the gift of God, not a result of works, so that no one may boast."

## Anyone can be saved:

Romans 10:13

"For everyone who calls on the name of the Lord will be saved."

The beauty of the Gospel is that Jesus took on the full weight of our sins. He died in our place. We cannot earn our salvation, neither do we deserve it. Jesus paid the total price so that we can be forgiven and enter into eternal life. He died and rose again with the power to defeat both sin and death!

*He died so that we might live!*

One of the last things Jesus said as He was dying on the cross was, "It is finished." He did what we could never do ourselves. It is such an amazing gift from God through His unparalleled love for us. It is wonderful to not only share God's Word with others, but also to experience Scripture come to life as we follow God in loving others. In Luke 11:34, we read:

> "Your eye is the lamp of your body. When your eye is healthy, your whole body is full of light, but when it is bad, your body is full of darkness."

As I continued to learn to love, I felt this Scripture verse about eyes and light become real in an amazing way. Later in this book, I will describe in more detail how God opened a door for me to enter prisons to help minister to inmates. One day as I was entering a maximum-security prison for my weekly visit to death row, a prison warden was going through the security check point at the same time as me.

We spoke briefly in the lobby. I introduced myself and shared which unit I served in. The warden said, "Yes, that's great what you have been doing in Unit Two (death row), but we really need an outreach started in Unit Four (solitary confinement). Nobody wants to go there." I said something like, "Ok, I'll pray about it."

Upon inquiring to the prison chaplain, it turned out that Unit Four was the most violent unit in the prison. It has the highest assault rates, both inmate-to-inmate assaults and inmate-to-officer assaults. The chaplain shared that these inmates were mostly on solitary confinement with certain selected times of the day allowed out of their cell for a time in the middle of the pod of cells. I told him I was willing to go there, so he prayed over me and off we went. The chaplain personally escorted me from his office to the unit by using his walkie talkie to communicate with the control center and with his set of keys to open doors.

As we finally approached the door of Unit Four, he communicated with the officer in the control center and we were electronically buzzed in. Then we walked up to another door with bars. The chaplain unlocked it, and I walked in. To my surprise, he did not follow me in and instead locked the door behind me, turned around and walked away. I immediately realized that even the chaplain was not willing to enter this unit.

I started visiting inmates one cell at a time. One of the inmates asked who had let me in and I responded that the chaplain had. The Lord was with me as I visited these inmates, going cell to cell. I offered prayer support, listened intently, and read Scripture verses as the conversations led in various directions.

I will never forget what transpired next. I clearly remember being on the second level of the unit, visiting one cell at a time. I approached one cell at the corner of the second level toward the end of the evening. There stood an inmate looking at me through a narrow window on his cell door. He looked intently at me as I approached. He saw the Bible in my hand and began to taunt me. He said, "Do you have a satanic bible?" I said, "What?" He responded, "You heard me. I said, do you have a satanic bible? I am the devil."

At that moment I could have responded in many ways. I could have walked past his cell, knowing that he was not welcoming me. However, it was at that very moment that God stopped me right there. God gave me a supernatural sense of His love for this man. I just stood there and stared at him. It felt as if I was beaming the love of Jesus as we both stared at each other intently in the eyes. This went on for quite a few seconds, as if time were standing still.

Finally, after the long pause, I noticed his face begin to crack with emotion. Immediately, God gave me words for him. I said, "I get it. You will never know peace until you know Jesus." He responded with great emotion, "Look at me! I'm a gangbanger in prison. I ain't coming to know no Jesus!" Instantly, God gave me more words for him. I shared that none of us is good enough for God's grace. That Jesus paid for our sins and when we receive Him, God comes in and cleans us up from the inside out. It was only mere minutes later that we were bowing our heads in prayer for him to dedicate his life to the Lord.

*It is the love of Christ that compels us.*

Years ago, when I first moved to Nashville, I found out about a homeless ministry that occurred regularly underneath a bridge near downtown. I would join in the ministry efforts there as often as possible. There was free food, free groceries and toiletries, Bibles given out, and even a worship service with preaching right out in the open. One day, I was there in the back of a large crowd of people listening to the worship and message being preached. As I stood back there, the Lord showed me a man about twenty feet in front of me, also near the back, and prompted me to go pray for him.

For some reason, this intimidated me. I thought of all the reasons I did not need to go approach this man. I thought I could pray for him from afar, so I did. As I was praying, the Lord brought the following words from Matthew 25:40 to mind very clearly:

> "And the King will answer them, 'Truly, I say to you, as you did it to one of the least of these my brothers, you did it to me.'"

I was immediately convicted. I realized by not being obedient, it was as if I was directly not loving the Lord. I quickly relented and walked up to the man. He drew his attention away from the service and looked at me. I told him that the Lord told me to come to pray for him. I asked how I could pray for him and he shared that he was trying to quit using drugs. I laid a hand on his shoulder and prayed for his deliverance. He was very thankful for the prayer, and I went on my way.

Later that evening I walked back to my car, still thinking about God's grace in my life in helping me to be truly obedient in serving and loving others as unto Him. I drove away from the bridge and back toward downtown. About a mile into my drive, I felt prompted to look out of the left window and across the street into a crowd of people. To my surprise, I spotted the same man I had prayed for earlier. In that instant he locked eyes with me and waved with gratitude. God was reminding me that He sees everything.

*God's love for us is so great!*

# Chapter 3

## Trusting God for Fruit

As I learned, sometimes conversations do not always go as planned, but it is essential to remain obedient through the process and trust God alone for the fruit. It is God who draws people to Christ. Jesus said directly, as recorded in John 6:44:

> "No one can come to me unless the Father who sent me draws him. And I will raise him up on the last day."

On a flight from Nashville, Tennessee to Chicago, Illinois, I was sitting at a window seat on the plane. An older lady sat in the middle, and an unrelated older man sat next to her on the aisle seat. The plane took off, and I had my laptop out in front of me. The Lord prompted me to offer a Bible to the lady next to me, so I reached down in my laptop bag and got one out. I looked over to her, smiling, and said, "I have a gift for you; it is a copy of God's Word." She responded, "No, thanks, I'm a Jehovah's Witness." I said, "Ok, no problem," and reached down to put the Bible back in my bag.

At that point, I could have been discouraged and taken the rejection personally. However, I decided to keep praying and gave it over to the Lord. I kept the conversation going with her and found out she was passing through Chicago for a layover on her way to New York City.

When she mentioned New York City, I excitedly shared that I have been blessed to visit there many times. I told her how honored I was to deliver Bibles to the firemen in the city. As soon as I said the word "firemen," the older man next to her leaned forward and looked at me. He said, "I am a volunteer fireman!"

He then shared that he was heading to Chicago to visit his terminally ill sister. I told him I was sorry to hear about his sister. He shared that she was a born-again Christian who had been witnessing to him for many years. He said he was personally reluctant to become a Christian because he loved to drink a lot of alcohol. I then shared the Good News with him. Afterward, I reached back down in my laptop bag and pulled out the Bible. I opened it and showed him where he could find comfort in God's Word through difficult times. The lady in the middle was listening and watching the whole time. He gladly accepted the Bible.

Then the lady in the middle seat unexpectedly asked me a surprising question. She said, "Do you have another Bible?" I said yes and reached down and pulled another one out of my laptop bag. She received it and shared that she was heading to New York City to attend her sister's funeral. I told her that I hoped God's Word would encourage her as well. I asked them both if I could pray for them, and they agreed. After the prayer in mid-flight, the man leaned forward and said, "I don't think it was by accident that both of us sat next to you on this flight today." I agreed, and then prayed internally as the lady read Scriptures for the remainder of the flight.

As we deboarded the plane, the man and I continued a bit of conversation. He said he would continue to think about becoming a Christian. I encouraged him that it was the best thing he could ever do, and then told him that I was sure his terminally ill sister would be honored to pray with him to receive Christ. Even after an initial rejection, I am so glad I decided to fully trust God for the fruit and continue to love on these people right where they were.

At this point, you might be wondering why I always look for an opportunity to give someone a Bible when I have the chance. It is simply because God honors His Word. The Word of God is powerful to speak to people. It provides answers to critical life questions, and it also can provide help, comfort, and direction for people during their time of need. Here are a few Scripture verses describing the power and importance of the Word itself:

Hebrews 4:12

"For the word of God is living and active, sharper than any two-edged sword, piercing to the division of soul and of spirit, of joints and of marrow, and discerning the thoughts and intentions of the heart."

Isaiah 40:8

"The grass withers, the flower fades,
    but the word of our God will stand forever."

Isaiah 55:11

"so shall my word be that goes out from my mouth;
    it shall not return to me empty,
but it shall accomplish that which I purpose,
    and shall succeed in the thing for which I sent it."

John 17:17

"Sanctify them in the truth; your word is truth."

On another occasion, I was in New York City on the streets of midtown Manhattan. Just a few blocks over from Times Square, I was blessed to be giving out Bibles and ministering to people on the sidewalk. I got down to my last Bible and began to look around. As I saw the hordes of people all around me and realized I only had one Bible left, I felt insignificant and thought to myself, "What real difference can I make?" At that very moment, I felt the Lord speak to me, saying, "Don't you realize what you have in your hand?"

I realized I had the most powerful possession one could have on this earth. Upon conviction from God and with a renewed zeal, I prayed "Ok God, just show me who to give this to, and I will." After a few moments, God showed me an older lady sitting alone on a park bench. I knew instantly: "*her*."

I walked over to her and sat down nearby. After making conversation about the weather, I pulled out the Bible and told her I had a gift. I showed her God's Word and encouraged her that she could find help in her time of need. For some reason, the word "suicide" came to light. I was caught a bit off-guard to point out the topic of suicide with someone I had just met, but then I began to share with her about God's love for her.

She then shared something I would never have imagined. She said, "I live alone. At night, I see visions of demons telling me to kill myself." I told her that giving her life to the Lord was the best thing she could do. Right there on the bench, we prayed for her to receive Jesus and be delivered from the demonic attacks of thoughts of suicide. Afterward, she looked at me in awe and said, "How in the world did you know to come and talk to me about that?" I said, "I didn't know, but God did. All I did was say a prayer, and He directed me to you." She realized God's love for her that day in a special way. To God be the glory!

Again, sometimes conversations do not always go as planned, but it is vital to remain in obedience to the Lord through the process and trust God alone for the fruit. One day I was in sunny southern California in Los Angeles, out on a sidewalk in Venice Beach. There is a lot of beautiful scenery there, but also a lot of drug use and homeless people. I prayed that God would show me whom to minister to and offer a copy of His Word. He brought to my attention a young lady with blond hair that was in dreadlocks. I immediately got the feeling that she would not want a Bible. I went back and forth with the Lord on this. He continued to press me: "*her.*"

I relented, and in obedience through prayer, by faith, I approached her. She smiled, and I offered her a Bible, telling her of God's love for her. She said, "What's that?" I told her it was a Bible. She looked at it, then physically jumped back, saying "No way, get that away from me!" I responded, "Ok, no problem" and then she walked away.

I learned a valuable lesson about obedience that day. Despite her reaction, I knew that God was pursuing her. He was allowing me to be a small cog in the wheel of His love story for her. I was honored and thankful for the reminder that only true fruit comes from Him. My job was to be obedient and reach out through His love. It also allowed me to see where she was spiritually in the moment so I could pray specifically for her.

*God is faithful.*

I certainly praise God for His faithfulness as we reach out to others with the Good News. In Luke 14:23, Jesus tells us a parable of a master preparing a banquet,

> "And the master said to the servant, 'Go out to the highways and hedges and compel people to come in, that my house may be filled.'"

Sometimes those highways and hedges look daunting and we can doubt the receptivity of those we are "compelling to come." One such time I was in MacArthur Park near downtown Los Angeles. I will share in a later chapter how God first called me to minister to people in MacArthur Park. This park is notorious for drug activity and homelessness. On this occasion I was walking through the park giving out Bibles and praying with people. I walked nearby a stretch of the park that was lined with homeless tents. As I walked by, I continued in prayer and asked God to show me to whom to offer a Bible.

At that moment, I looked down and saw a young couple. The young man was smoking something out of a pipe. I felt the Lord prompt me to approach him. I thought to myself that there was no way this man would take a Bible. However, out of obedience to God I reached out my hand and offered him God's Word. To my surprise, he willingly received it. I was reminded in that moment of God's love for everyone as He pursues them right where they are.

*Who are we to judge people from outside appearances when God is looking at the heart?*

This occurred another time as I was walking the streets of New Orleans, Louisiana with a bag of Bibles and praying for God to lead the way. God opened many opportunities to give people a word of encouragement along with the gift of His Word. I distinctly remember walking through an area near the French Quarter known as Jackson Square, a historical landmark and park.

Right in front of an old church were many people out relaxing on benches and walking around. There were also several tables set up where people were conducting Tarot card readings. As I walked by, I felt the Lord prompt me to offer the Tarot card readers His Word. Again, I thought they would not be open to receiving the Bibles but to my surprise, two out of three of them accepted it.

*Thank God for giving us the grace to trust Him.*

# Chapter 4

## *Learning to Hear God's Voice*

After I surrendered my life to the Lord, I knew right away that if I really did not want to waste any more time like I had been doing, then I would need to get to know the voice of God. I did not want to do things that I thought were good by my standards; I wanted to make sure I was doing what God wanted me to do.

Immediately after my encounter with His forgiveness and saving grace, I began to speak to God. I would hear Him respond softly in the Spirit. As He spoke, He would confirm it by allowing me to sense His nearness through the Holy Spirit. Learning to discern the voice of God and the will of God became of utmost importance in my life.

Allow me to slow down a minute here. You may be reading so far and have no idea what I am talking about, so let us break it down. First, do not feel bad if you do not understand what I have been saying about God and being saved. It would not be out of line for you to think that this guy must be crazy; after all, he is talking about hearing from God, isn't he?

*Could this even be possible?*

Please let me tell you with all my heart that the answer is, "yes." God can certainly make Himself known to us, and it is wonderful to know that He is not far off at any time. In the Bible, the Apostle Paul told the Athenians in the book of Acts, chapter 17, this very thing:

"[22] So Paul, standing in the midst of the Areopagus, said: "Men of Athens, I perceive that in every way you are very religious. [23] For as I passed along and observed the objects of your worship, I found also an altar with this inscription: 'To the unknown god.' What therefore you worship as unknown, this I proclaim to you. [24] The God who made the world and everything in it, being Lord of heaven and earth, does not live in temples made by man, [25] nor is he served by human hands, as though he needed anything, since he himself gives to all mankind life and breath and everything. [26] And he made from one man every nation of mankind to live on all the face of the earth, having determined allotted periods and the boundaries of their dwelling place, [27] that they should seek God, and perhaps feel their way toward him and find him. Yet he is actually not far from each

28

one of us, ²⁸ for 'In him we live and move and have our being'; as even some of your own poets have said, 'For we are indeed his offspring.'"

Paul was used by God mightily to make Him known, and he boldly proclaimed that He is "actually not far from each one of us." Therefore, the first thing to recognize is that God is near to us at this very moment. There is absolutely nothing hidden from Him, and He understands all things. In Psalm 139 we also read:

"Where can I go from your Spirit?
    Where can I flee from your presence?
⁸ If I go up to the heavens, you are there;
    if I make my bed in the depths, you are there.
⁹ If I rise on the wings of the dawn,
    if I settle on the far side of the sea,
¹⁰ even there your hand will guide me,
    your right hand will hold me fast.
¹¹ If I say, "Surely the darkness will hide me
    and the light become night around me,"
¹² even the darkness will not be dark to you;
    the night will shine like the day,
    for darkness is as light to you.

¹³ For you created my inmost being;
    you knit me together in my mother's womb.
¹⁴ I praise you because I am fearfully and wonderfully made;
    your works are wonderful,
    I know that full well.
¹⁵ My frame was not hidden from you
    when I was made in the secret place,
    when I was woven together in the depths of the earth.

[16] Your eyes saw my unformed body;
   all the days ordained for me were written in your
book
     before one of them came to be.
[17] How precious to me are your thoughts, God!
     How vast is the sum of them!
[18] Were I to count them,
     they would outnumber the grains of sand—
     when I awake, I am still with you."

How wonderful is it to know that God knows us fully, He understands us completely, and He is not far away from each of us! He knows the depths of our being even more than we do ourselves. He is the creator and sustainer of our very being. As such, we should not be afraid to talk to Him by faith, knowing that He actually hears us.

I wonder if many people miss the blessing of allowing God to speak back...if they would only listen. If we need to discern the voice of God, then we can simply ask Him to help us know and recognize His voice in our lives. This is a growing process, and we should not hesitate to continually ask Him to make His voice clear in a way that we will know it is Him.

Once I began to discern God's voice in my own life, I wanted to know Him more and more. To do that, I had to draw near to Him no matter the cost. I would pray and fast, and fast and pray. I began to select something that I did most every day and chose to fast from it, sometimes for even a month at a time. This would include things like eating no desserts or eating no meat for a whole month as I earnestly prayed for God to make His voice clear in my life.

This was not about creating some sort of ritual, but more so about creating a personal discipline for me to help focus myself on intentionally drawing close to God. I was learning to deny other things so I could focus more and prioritize my relationship with God. Through this process of seeking God with intentional disciplines like prayer and fasting, God began to speak to me, teaching me about His character and helping me to understand areas of my life in which I needed to grow so I could bear fruit. We see this concept in the following Scripture verses:

John 15:5

"I am the vine, you are the branches. He who abides in Me, and I in him, bears much fruit; for without Me you can do nothing."

1 Peter 1:23-25

"Since you have been born again, not of perishable seed but of imperishable, through the living and abiding word of God; [24] for

'All flesh is like grass
    and all its glory like the flower of grass.
The grass withers,
    and the flower falls,
[25] but the word of the Lord remains forever.'

And this word is the good news that was preached to you."

*I found that learning to abide in Him through His Word and His presence was the only way to truly bear fruit in life.*

# Chapter 5

## *Divine Appointments*

Early on, as I was discovering how to walk by faith, I remember praying for God to use me for His glory in sharing the Good News with others. Even though this was not something I was accustomed to, I knew it was very important in light of eternity. One day, I asked God to show me whom He would have me speak to during a busy day at the office. At that time, I was a small business owner, and on my lunch break, after praying that prayer I went across the street to a grocery store to get a sandwich.

When I walked into the grocery store my eyes were wide open, scanning the crowd and looking intently for whom God might want me to speak with. However, I never felt a prompting, so I got my sandwich, continued to look around, and then went to check out. I walked out of the grocery store toward my car feeling a bit discouraged. I began to wonder if I missed my opportunity.

Maybe I did not listen hard enough to God. Maybe He just did not have a divine appointment for me that day. It was at this very moment, as I was feeling discouraged, that I went to lift my car door handle when I felt prompted to turn around. I immediately locked eyes with a man walking out of the grocery store. He must have been more than 100 feet away. But I instantly knew: *"him."*

I grabbed a small Bible and began to walk toward him. I became nervous and asked God to use me despite my weaknesses and shortfalls. As I approached the man, who was by then a row of cars over in the parking lot, I tapped him on the back of his shoulder. He turned around and looked at me with a questioning face that appeared to say, "What do you want?" so I simply said, "I have a gift for you. It's a copy of God's Word. I want you to know that God loves you. We all have sinned, but God made a remedy for that sin by sending Jesus to die on the cross for us. Anybody can receive Jesus as Savior. I just want you to have this." He said, "okay" and took the Bible.

I felt relieved that he took the Bible. It was at this moment that I felt prompted by God to keep going, so I asked, "Have you ever done that before? Have you ever prayed to receive Jesus as your Savior?" He said, "no," and then he shared that he tried to live his life right and treat others with respect. I responded by encouraging him that receiving Jesus was the best thing he could ever do. Then, I felt prompted to keep going, so I said, "It is totally up to you, but I am here if you would like to pray to receive Christ."

I will never forget the look on his face. He looked down at the Bible and took a long moment to reflect hard. His eyebrows wadded up as he was deep in thought. Then, after the long pause, he looked up at me and said "Okay, let's do it."

It was at that moment, in the middle of a grocery store parking lot, with cars driving by and people pushing their grocery carts, that we bowed our heads and prayed for him to receive Christ as his Savior. I could sense the presence of God in a mighty way. Afterward, he looked at me and said something else I hope to never forget. He said, "You have no idea how long I have needed to do that." I gave him a big hug and left.

As I drove away, I saw him out of my car window and he shouted, "Thank you!" I returned to my office and after I parked, I just sat in my car and prayed for this man. I could not believe what had just happened. I learned an incredible lesson that day. The man's words rang out in my mind: "You have no idea how long I have needed to do that!"

*He was right; I did not know. Yet, God did.*

It was not about me. It was about God's redemptive work in his life as God was pursuing him. My job was to be faithful and respond to God's leading as a vessel for

His glory. I learned that it was not about me trying to convince anybody about the Gospel, but rather letting God simply use me as He was drawing someone to Himself.

Another time, soon after this, I began to ask God to help me to hear from Him on a deeper level. On a late Saturday evening, I began a fast to grow closer to the Lord. I fervently prayed that the fast would be honoring to God. The next morning, I went to church as usual.

After church, I drove to downtown Charlotte with a bag full of Bibles. I parked at the top of the 7$^{th}$ street station parking garage and walked to the edge of the roof, overlooking the Charlotte skyline. As I looked down at the people on the streets, I prayed that God would direct my steps to share the Gospel with those whom he wanted me to.

I went down to the street level and began to walk and pray. God began to open opportunities for me to share His Word. I distinctly remember one homeless man with whom I began to share Christ. He was an older man and his face had scars on both cheeks. He responded to the Gospel, and we began to pray together for him to receive Christ.

At that very moment, a younger man came walking up, and I sensed the Holy Spirit move me to begin a conversation with him. I immediately asked him if he knew Christ, and he responded that he was not sure. I tried to give him a Bible, but he said he already had one and pulled a ragged looking little Bible from his back pocket.

I shared with him that knowing Jesus as Lord was the most important part of this life to ensure he was saved by grace through faith. After sharing the Gospel, the young man bowed his head and prayed earnestly to receive Christ as his Savior, and to surrender his life to the Lord. Afterward, he looked greatly relieved and began to share his story with me. I was stunned by what he said.

He shared that he was not from Charlotte. In fact, he had just recently taken a bus down from New York to try to reconnect with his girlfriend. He shared that she had recently gotten pregnant and after he got in town, he found out that the baby was not his. He then shared he had a rough life and was even abused as a child. He said everything in life was going wrong, and he had lost hope. He told me that he decided as a last hope he would attend church that morning. He said at the church service nobody acknowledged him, and he felt so alone.

Leaving the church service discouraged and hopeless from all the pain he was enduring, he decided it was too much to handle and that he wanted to end his life that day. He took out that little ragged Bible, looked up at the sky and cursed God, and then threw the Bible against one of the tall downtown buildings. He realized people were looking at him, so he picked up the Bible and stuck it in his back pocket. As he was walking around downtown Charlotte, he began to look for a place to commit suicide. He pulled out a drawstring from his jacket hood to strangle himself.

He thought to himself that he did not want to do it out in the open on the sidewalk, or even in an alleyway. Then he thought there must be some parks in Charlotte. He then saw an imaginary vision of himself committing suicide on a park bench, and then he saw another imaginary vision of a news article with the heading, "Man Kills Himself in Park." He asked a bystander for directions to the closest park and was told there was one only a few blocks away. He began walking in the direction toward the park...when as God would have it, I was standing there ready for God's divine appointment.

*Little did I know he was mere steps away from committing suicide.*

After hearing him share the story, he showed me the drawstring with which he was going to strangle himself. I told him that God loved him and had a wonderful plan for his life. We prayed again together, and I rejoiced at God's amazing grace and sovereign hand. To God be the glory!

I cannot help but wonder how many people like this young man are walking all around us in our daily lives. People are hurting even to the point of death, and we have the most glorious Good News to share with them.

*The question becomes: are we simply willing to be vessels useful for the kingdom of God?*

This very type of learning to hear from God during daily activities became routine, and often even unexpected. Recently, I dropped off a rental car at the airport and needed to take a taxi back home. As I got into the back of the car, I greeted the driver with a few words, and he began to drive. As usual, I proceeded to check emails on my phone when I heard a prompting from the Lord to, "pay attention." This was again in the form of what many describe as a "still small voice," as God whispered to me in the Spirit.

I responded in obedience, putting my phone in my pocket, and then started paying attention to what the Lord was doing. The driver asked me where I had come from, so I shared that I was dropping off a car for recent ministry work I had done. I mentioned the word, Bible, and he said, "Yes, I am familiar with the Bible. I am from Nepal and most of my family are Hindu, but I have been thinking about becoming a Christian." I could not believe what I just heard, so I began to share the Good News!

The rest of the way home, I felt the Lord tell me to just get to know him. We talked about many things, including his hobbies of traveling and playing soccer. When we pulled up to my house, I asked him if I could pray with him. He replied, "Yes." It was at that moment I felt compelled to share the Gospel with him again. Afterward, I looked at him and said that it was completely between him and God, but I was available to pray with him if he was ready to receive Jesus as his Savior. He thought for a moment and said, "yes." We then bowed our heads as he prayed to receive Christ and trust Him as his personal Savior.

I felt like I was floating walking back into the house. It was so humbling that I could hardly hold back the tears.

It is a truly marvelous feeling to be used by God, and I could not help but to feel so unworthy.

*Praise God for His grace as He prompts us to "pay attention" to His divine appointments!*

# Chapter 6

## Walking Through Open Doors

Throughout my journey, God has opened so many doors for me to walk through by faith. As I have spent time reflecting on them, some are even hard for me to believe, if I had not experienced them firsthand. It has been amazing watching God work mightily through my weaknesses and fears, as I have had to desperately seek His presence and walk through them by faith in many cases.

As God has led me in service for His Kingdom work, He has shown Himself mighty and victorious to carry me through—despite the circumstances. We read in the

Bible an example of the concept of open doors in 1
Corinthians 16:9:

> "For a wide door for effective work has opened to
> me…"

I can remember my very first trip to New York City. God
had opened the door for me to go there on a mission
trip in the fall of 2009 and I was both excited and
nervous. I remember being on the plane during the
flight there and thinking, "Wow this is a huge city." I
did not know how I would be able to handle whatever
was going to come my way. I was planning to join a
team and give away a lot of Bibles.

Beforehand, I did not even have the money to go.
Therefore, I sold some of my old DJ equipment to a
friend of mine. He gave me $1,000 cash, and I vividly
remember driving away. It was a rainy day, and looking
through the water on the windshield as the wipers went
back and forth, I just looked up to the sky and told God,
"I'm going to take this $1,000 dollars, go to New York
City and help distribute Your Word."

On the plane, there was a young woman next to me
who had flown back and forth from Charlotte to New
York City regularly. She said, "Don't worry, New York
City is just another big city like any other city." I
landed at John F. Kennedy Airport and had to catch a
bus over to LaGuardia Airport to finally get to a nearby
hotel in Queens. Funny enough, it turned out I did not
even book my tickets to the right airport.

When I got to the hotel parking lot, I saw three tractor
trailers full of Bibles. Together they contained about

half a million Scriptures. My eyes were opened to the move of God that was going to happen in the city of New York that next week.

Can you imagine seeing stacks and stacks of Bibles, amounting to almost 500,000 copies? That is a lot of Bibles. All I could do in the moment was pray over the people that were about to receive those Scriptures.

I got up very early each day, finding myself traveling to a whole new part of the city; from Brooklyn to Rikers Island, from the Bronx to Roosevelt Island. We even spent time in Manhattan. It was amazing!

As the teams of volunteers were grouping together to go out into the city, one of the team leaders, named Trevor, stood up and made a special announcement. He said, "I am needing someone to come with me to visit homeless shelters in some of the worst neighborhoods in the city." I stood up and walked up to him, saying I would go.

He saw that I was young and stared at me for a long moment, and so I simply stared back at him. After he realized I was serious about going along, he agreed and off we went. It was such a blessing visiting the shelters and ministering to many of the city's homeless population. Trevor and I immediately became friends.

During this trip was also my first experience walking into Rikers Island Jail. I was feeling so nervous as we had to get clearance to go over the bridge and onto the island. Rikers Island is home to one of the world's largest correctional institutions and happens to also be one of the toughest jails in the world. It houses

43

thousands and thousands of inmates. We went through all the different security checks, and the doors closed behind us. We made it in, and I remember being in this empty chapel room just praying and feeling nervous and asking God to take over.

We were given an opportunity to lead a chapel service for the inmates. I was at the front of the chapel praying when the first inmate came walking in. He had handcuffs on with a bar in between them so he was completely locked in. He also had on mitts covering his hands so he could not have access to his fingers. Even with the mitts, the handcuffs, and the bar attachment, he was a threat to hurt other inmates or himself.

As he walked in, the guard began to take off the handcuffs and there was another corrections officer standing by with a video camera. The officer said in a direct tone, "State your first and last name, sir." The inmate then looked directly into the camera and stated his name. I remember just thinking, "Wow, look at these maximum-security inmates coming into this room with us!"

Before long, the room began to fill up and we had about two dozen inmates in there. There were only four of us volunteers to help with the chapel service. I was one of the first guys up to the podium to talk to them, and it was an incredible experience! God completely took over and gave me a sense of boldness.

I looked at them and said, "You're probably sitting here wondering what this young guy is doing here." At that time, I was twenty-six years old. I shared my testimony of how God had saved, delivered, healed, and set me free. Then, He set me on-fire for Him. I could sense the move of the power of the presence of God in that room.

I had never experienced so much nervousness combined with an intense, comforting, and refreshing move of the Holy Spirit. I was surprised as those inmates began to worship and praise God. I remember all four of our volunteer messages lined up back-to-back. We had no script, but God aligned the messages perfectly. What a glorious time.

That afternoon we went to another part of the jail. We entered an old dilapidated gym that was no longer in use. This section housed the younger offenders. They probably had lighter sentencing for the crimes they had committed. This time we had about 100-150 guys in the room. Again, getting to speak to them about the freedom that they could have in Christ, about having a genuine relationship with God, and to encourage them, was overwhelming.

It was beyond my wildest imagination as I got a glimpse of how God pursues everyone. I remember leaving that day never being the same, feeling emboldened and empowered by the Holy Spirit and how God was so faithful to give me that confidence even while experiencing nervousness with the unknowns of something new. Learning to simply walk by faith and not by sight, I realized how the Lord had honored that. The highlight of my entire year was going into that facility.

That same week, I found myself in Queens' Chinatown, helping give out several thousand copies of God's Word in the Korean and Chinese languages. We did this on a sidewalk in Queens where many roads intersected, and buses were dropping off people. Just to see the sea of faces was incredible. I began to engage with people there on the street. I had prayed so diligently that God would give me an opportunity to lead someone to the Lord that week.

As I looked out into the crowd, amid all the Asian people walking down the sidewalk comes a Middle Eastern man. He stopped, and I talked with him and shared the Gospel. I told him that God loved him, that we were all sinners, and God made the way of reconciliation by giving His son Jesus as a ransom for our sins. I remember looking at him and saying, "Brother, you can receive Jesus at any time. Are you ready? We can pray."

He said, "Yes, of course. Let's pray." We prayed right then and there in the middle of the sidewalk, in the busyness of Chinatown, for him to receive Jesus Christ as his Lord and Savior. I could not believe it! I gave him a copy of Scripture. He went walking off, and I thought that I was in the middle of a dream because that could not possibly have just happened. It was amazing to see how in New York City things can happen so quickly. The opportunities are abounding.

Later the same week, I found myself in a nursing home in Brooklyn giving out Scriptures, going room by room. As I walked down the hallway, I remember God telling me specifically, "Do not just give out my Word, tell them about my Word. Talk. Speak."

So, I took a stack of Scriptures and went down a long corridor. I will never forget going down that hall telling people, "Hey, do you know Jesus?" "Do you know Jesus?" "Yes, yes." "Good, praise God!" I was simply encouraging those that were in that nursing home.

I finally got to the very back room on the right-hand side of that hallway. What transpired is something I will never forget. There were two old women in the room. I walked up to the first one and said, "Ma'am, I would like to give you a copy of God's word," and she said, "Oh no, it's fine I already have one." She pointed to her nightstand where there was a big copy of the Bible there. I said, "Oh, okay great! Praise the Lord!"

Then, I went over to her roommate. What I saw was this little old woman on her bed, which was like a cot on the floor. I kneeled down with a big smile and said, "Ma'am, I have a gift for you. It's a copy of God's Word, and I'd like to give this you." She stared blankly at my face as I said, "You know God loves you very much and He sent His Son Jesus so that you can receive Him. I hope that you will. It's the best thing that you can ever do."

I looked at her in the face, and as she looked at me blankly, I began to wonder if she was even coherent. I wondered if she had Alzheimer's disease or dementia. She was just this little old woman on the floor in this bed. As she looked up at me, she opened her mouth and said something to me that I could have never, ever imagined. She looked up at me and replied, "I spent my entire life convincing others that I was God."

Instantly, it was almost as if God gave me the words right out of my mouth to say to her. Without even a blink, I said with a smile, "Ma'am, I know that you think you've done a lot of bad things in your life, but God is bigger than that, and He can forgive you...if you are willing to receive the forgiveness that He has for you in Christ Jesus. Would you like to receive that forgiveness today?" She looked up at me and immediately said, "Yes, I would." I said, "Amen, let's pray."

We prayed together for her to receive Jesus as her Lord and Savior, and asked God to forgive her. After we prayed that prayer, I gave her the copy of God's Word and I told her, "Read this, it's going to tell you all about Jesus." As I walked out of that room, I felt like I was floating down the hallway. I was experiencing this unbelievable feeling of euphoria, and I knew that even if God had brought me all the way to New York City just for this one woman, it was all worth it. Glory to God!

*God blesses us with divine appointments as we endeavor to simply follow Him through open doors.*

One little old woman, on the floor, in a bed, in a nursing home, in Brooklyn. I was astounded. Not only had God given me that opportunity, but He gave me the words to say in the moment. That was the key for me to remember: God is the one in control and our job is just to be faithful and obedient as the Lord leads, guides, prompts and directs. We need to be willing to listen to the Lord and respond to His leading. It comes back to learning how to simply abide in Him. What an honor and a growth experience that simple moment was for me!

On one early morning that same week, I was in Brooklyn at the University of Long Island. It was a bitter cold day in October, and I remember that my hands were freezing. It was seven o'clock in the morning and I stood out on the sidewalk. Two other volunteers had gone to the front of the school and were giving out Scriptures there as the students went inside. They had set me up at the very back by myself. There was a little gated back entrance and a fence. I began to think, "Well, I guess some of the students may come in this back way."

Little did I know as the hours went by that because it was the only entrance in the back of the school, most of the students went through that way. Not only was this the case, but they all had to funnel in right by me— since the rest of the entrance was gated. Literally, this made for the most wonderful opportunity to give away a massive number of Bibles. I think I gave away a little over 600 Bibles that morning, standing there by that small back entrance. As I was giving them out, I was thinking about the verses in Psalms and humming praises to God as I thought about His grace for simply allowing me to be there and give out His Word.

As the hours went on, a delivery truck came by and began to drop off some items right next to me in that back entrance. A professor walked by. She began to shout, "Do not pass out religious literature! Do not pass out religious literature here!" She was shouting very loudly over the students who were going in the entrance between where she and I stood. It was so loud the delivery guys stopped and stared. It was such a scene.

Without skipping a beat, I continued to give out the Bibles. I had no words to say to her except, "Ma'am have a great day!" As she went storming off, I felt a little bit intimidated and began to step back a little bit from my aggressive spot right by that gated entrance. I stepped back maybe a foot or two. I thought, "Here I am, my first time in New York City in Brooklyn, and I am not sure what is going to happen."

After maybe five minutes went by, a security guard came walking up and said that he had a complaint. I immediately recognized what he meant and said, "Yeah, I believe it's that woman ...that professor." He said, "Yes, that's correct. She said that you were standing out here giving out religious literature."

As he was talking, I just kept giving more Bibles to the students as they walked on by. He looked down at me, and he looked closely at the Bibles in my hand. Then he looked back at me and said, "Well, you know what that is don't you?" Without even beginning to know what he was going to say, expecting the worst scenario, I said, "What's that?" He said, "That's nothing but the devil trying to stop you because that's not religious literature. That's the Word of God." As the Holy Spirit moved, this overwhelming comforting sensation came upon me and I looked at him and said, "Praise God!"

I made sure he had a copy of God's Word before he went walking away. God had sent that security guard to not only communicate what happened with the professor, but also to remind me that God had me there for a reason and a purpose. So, with a fully renewed sense of confidence, I stepped forward into my position to give out God's Word to all those students.

Again, it did not go smoothly all the time, but God was faithful. One student grabbed one of the Bibles and threw it in the trash can just inside the entrance. I went over and picked it out. Continuing, that same week I found myself at a street fair in Long Island giving out hundreds of Bibles. It was great. I must have personally given out thousands of Bibles in a short week's time in New York City.

Long story short: So many experiences in that small amount of time, in that one-week mission trip, God revealed glimpses of His character repeatedly. His faithfulness, His Grace, and His all-sufficiency were apparent. He knows it all, and He used this experience to grow me in my walk with Him.

I learned that my job was to simply be faithful, and as I would serve, God would reveal Himself. It grew me so deeply in my walk with Him because of the revelations of His grace, of His presence, of His sovereign power, and of His love. The depths of His mercy and the richness of His grace He was showing to others were undeniable.

From that point, I began to want to give more and more of my life to Him. As I went back home and reminisced, it was announced that over 480,000 copies of the Word of God had gone out in that single week. From that time on, I was hooked. I was absolutely hooked.

It was not about the number of Bibles, but the souls that God was reaching through the power of His Word. I have since gone back to New York City for a week every year for the last eleven years, all for the same reason. I hope to continue that trend for a long time to come. God is on the move in New York City. There is no doubt about it.

As I continue to reminisce on the ability of God to open doors, the following circumstance comes to mind. One day I was flying out of town when I felt prompted to look out of the airplane window. When I looked down, I saw a prison on the west side of town. I knew immediately that God was calling me to go into that prison. Therefore, I began to pray about it and ask God to open the door in His timing.

A while later when I was back in town, I followed through with my commitment to the Lord and attended a volunteer training certification event to become a volunteer for the prison. I continued to follow up after my paperwork was completed, but it took a full eight months before I was approved and cleared to take my picture for a volunteer badge which would give me access to the prison. This was the beginning of God calling me into a maximum-security prison ministry.

After I had my badge, I called the prison chaplain. I discovered that because eight months had passed from when I started the process, there was a new chaplain. I told him that I was a new volunteer with a brand-new badge and felt a call from God to go in and minister to the inmates. He said, "Great, but before I place you in a unit, I want to meet you so we can determine the best place for you." I said I would be glad to meet with him, so we set an appointment. I continued to pray and was eager for the appointment.

The day of the meeting with the chaplain, I got off work in the afternoon and drove across town through rush-hour traffic to the prison. Once I arrived, there was a shift change occurring for the corrections officers, so I had to wait in a long line of officers to go through the initial security check point. I learned that this was the highest-level maximum-security prison in the whole state, which houses the most violent offenders, as well as death row inmates.

After about an hour of going through security, I finally made it to the other side where an officer was sitting at a desk. I told him I had an appointment with the chaplain, and he got on his walkie-talkie to summon the chaplain. After a few minutes, he looked up at me and said, "I am sorry sir, but the chaplain has left the premises." I felt so discouraged, especially since I had driven all that way through traffic and had to wait an extended time to get through the security line.

Earlier, while I was in the lobby waiting to go through security, I found out that the death row inmates were housed in Unit Two. So, at that moment, with nothing to lose, I looked at the officer that was sitting at the desk and said "Well, since I am here, can I at least go into Unit Two to minister to the inmates?" Obviously, the officer knew exactly what Unit Two was. He stared at me right in the eyes. So, I stared right back at him in the eyes. The moment lingered for quite a while.

Then, after the awkward pause, he said "Go ahead." He must have been wanting to ensure that I was serious about my question. I said, "Great, do I need an officer escort?" He said, "No, just go through the gates and the officers will tell you where to go." I was thrilled and walked through my first steel door with nothing but my Bible and volunteer badge.

After I walked through the steel door, I saw a large fence with barbed wire spiraling on top of it. I walked up to the fence, heard a buzzing sound, and it began to slide open. I stepped past the first gated fence and it began to slide back closed behind me. I looked ahead and saw another large gated fence with barbed wire on top of it. I was now trapped in between these two fences. After another buzzing sound, the second fence gate began to slide open, and I stepped past it.

Then I proceeded to walk up to a building with a steel door. On the top of both sides of the door were a security camera and a light. After another buzzing sound, I pulled open the heavy steel door. I was met by an officer enclosed in a glass office. He asked that I slide my volunteer badge through an opening at the bottom of the window.

He looked at me to verify I was the same person as the picture on the badge, and then asked me to put my hand under a blacklight so he could see the invisible stamp on my hand. I had received this stamp on my hand earlier while going through the security check point. Then, after both security measures were verified, he waved for me to proceed into inner part of the prison.

At this point, I looked out and saw two more steel doors. I asked which one would lead me to Unit Two, and the officer pointed to the left one. After another buzzing sound, this steel door slid open from left to right. I continued my journey toward death row, steadfast in prayer while walking with a Bible in hand, praising God for this amazing open door to walk openly through this highest-level maximum-security prison. Ultimately, it took going through twelve steel doors that had to be electronically buzzed open by an officer in the control center to get where I was finally going.

As I approached the last steel door, I was met by another officer in an enclosed office with glass windows. This time, he was up high looking down on me. He never had seen me before, and I had never seen him before. He stared at me, then looked at my Bible in my hand, then looked back at me and waved me forward. The final steel door buzzed open and I entered the death row unit.

I could not believe what I saw. There I was, as the door opened, and in plain view I saw about twenty-four unrestrained death row inmates openly wandering around a day room. They were wearing white jumpsuits with big "TDOC" letters on them, which stands for Tennessee Department of Corrections. As I scanned the room, I was stunned that they were unrestrained...with no handcuffs or shackles of any kind. Then, I scanned the room again and realized that there were no officers in there, nor any other volunteers. It was just me and them. I imagine it must have been similar to what Daniel must have felt like walking into the lion's den.

About the time I realized all this, several of the inmates looked over at me as I stood in the doorway. I thought to myself, "Okay, Lord, here we go," and proceeded to walk into the middle of the room. After a few words with several inmates, they realized I had a Bible in my hand and so one inmate began to arrange some desks and chairs. I sat down with a few of the inmates and opened the Bible. This is what started a weekly Bible study in a death row unit that would go on for the next three years. God had opened the door to the most secure room, in the most secure prison, in the entire state.

I received amazing blessings through this act of obedience. Even that first day, I thought I was bringing Jesus into the prison, but He was already there waiting to meet me. One of the inmates shared that he was praying fervently for God to send a servant of God into the unit. It was about the time he was praying that God prompted me to look out of that airplane window.

That first day, those inmates shared a lot with me. One inmate taught me a lifelong lesson right away. He said, "I'm scheduled to be executed, but only God can determine when I go. And when that time is, I am ready." It is one thing to hear words like that from people in society, but to hear it from someone who was scheduled to be executed was powerful. The conviction in his eyes was so sincere. Since then, that man has been executed, and I am assured that he went to be with the Lord. What an amazing lesson and blessing!

I wish I could capture in these mere words the light that exists in the eyes of these saved inmates on death row. One inmate declared, "This isn't death row; this is life row!" It is truly amazing witnessing the power of the Gospel even amid such oppressed environments. I learned so much through this process. This part of my life, helping conduct a weekly Bible study for over three years in a death row unit, has been one of the highlights of my entire life.

Another time, God opened a door for me and a small team to enter a prison in Northwest Georgia named Hayes State Prison. At the time this occurred, Hayes State Prison was the most violent prison of all thirty-three state prisons in Georgia. In a four-week period, two inmates were killed in acts of violence and the prison was constantly on lockdown.

In fact, I was not even sure we would be allowed entrance on the day of our arrival. The team of volunteers and I circled for prayer as we entered the prison, asking God to lead the way. We met with the prison chaplain and he escorted us to the most secure part of the prison, where inmates were housed on full lockdown twenty-three hours a day.

I approached the first cell and looked at the inmate through a slim window. I had to speak with him through a crack in the door. I looked him in the eyes and began to share the Good News with him; that God loved him and sent His Son Jesus to die on the cross for him. I shared that he could have hope and forgiveness in Christ. He was ready to respond in faith. We bowed our heads and he prayed to receive Jesus as his Savior and to surrender his life to the Lord.

Afterward, I turned around and saw the eyes of the team and the chaplain. They were pleasantly amazed. They looked at me, looked at each other, then looked down at a cart full of Bibles, and we proceeded down the tier block of prison cells.

We subsequently visited 316 cells over the next five and a half hours and saw thirty-two inmates pray to receive Christ as their Savior! We had also given out hundreds of Bibles to those inmates. As we left the prison that day, the team was eager to return. I later found out that the prison chaplain was previously considering quitting his position, but that day he found a renewed vision for God's call on his life and remained faithful to fulfill his calling. Praise God!

*God leaves no stone unturned when it comes to getting His word where it needs to go.*

I had just left the death row unit of a maximum-security prison after ministering to the inmates in my home state when I received a text message from a friend about a music concert in town that evening. I immediately headed downtown to the city's biggest venue and connected with my friend. He happened to be the lead guitarist, named Brian, for the headlining band, Korn.

For those that may not be aware, Korn is a Grammy award winning, internationally renowned rock band, which also happened to be my favorite band growing up in high school. Although this band is known for its secular and hard rock music, several members of the band have received Christ in recent years.

Brian invited me backstage, where I followed him onto his tour bus parked in an underground area near the arena. As we sat on the tour bus, he introduced me to the bass guitar player of the band, named Fieldy. Brian asked me to share with Fieldy my testimony, and after sharing how God saved me, I concluded by highlighting that God had been opening many doors for me to walk through, including those of many prisons throughout the country. Fieldy responded by saying, "Yeah, this is also an unexpected place for you, huh?" I agreed that it was quite unusual to be on a tour bus of an internationally recognized band.

After we got off the bus, I prayed with several members of the band that God would open a door to minister to people that night at the concert. Both Brian and Fieldy agreed to have a meet-and-greet at the end of the show for the purpose of sharing their testimonies and the Gospel. Interestingly enough, the name of the tour was the "Welcome to Hell Tour," featuring Korn and Rob Zombie. I began to prayerfully scour the crowd to let people know of the private greeting event after the show. When the time came, there was a long line of fans that showed up to meet these members of the band.

Brian and Fieldy gathered the crowd and began to share their testimonies out loud, leading up to the Gospel message. They invited the crowd to respond and many hands went up, signaling a willingness to receive Christ. Amazingly, Brian and Fieldy led the group through a prayer to receive Jesus right there at the back of the venue. God opened doors for His Word to be proclaimed, even behind the scenes of a hard rock concert on a tour called "Welcome to Hell."

*God is faithful.*

Grace Upon Grace

# Chapter 7

## *Releasing Our Agenda for God's Agenda*

Earlier in the book, I made a reference to abiding in Christ to bear fruit. This basically means to fully yield our will for His, and ultimately trust Him for the outcome. Here is the more detailed portion of Scripture related to the subject:

John 15

"I am the true vine, and my Father is the vinedresser. [2] Every branch in me that does not bear fruit he takes away, and every branch that does bear fruit he prunes, that it may bear more fruit. [3] Already you are clean because of the word that I have spoken to you. [4] Abide in me, and I in you. As the branch cannot bear fruit by itself, unless it abides in the vine, neither can you, unless you abide in me. [5] I am the vine; you are the branches. Whoever abides in me and I in him, he it is that bears much fruit, for apart from me you can do nothing."

As the Scripture referenced above, Jesus said that apart from Him we cannot bear fruit. He clearly states that apart from Him we can do nothing. This is so reassuring in the aspect of us not having to feel the weight of the pressure on ourselves.

*It is God that does the work through us if we will simply yield to His will.*

During one of my mission trips to New York City, I started my day on the floor praying in the hotel room. I prayed that God would take over my day and lead me in the way He wanted me to go. After I got up off the floor my phone immediately began to ring. I answered the phone, and it was the organizer of our missions' outreach telling me he had a special assignment for me. I got excited as I had just prayed for God to lead me!

It was then that he shared he had gotten a phone call from a police commander in the Bronx who was very upset about some Bibles being dropped off there. He wanted someone to come and pick them up right away. I said okay and then began to worry about what I might say to a very angry police commander in one of the toughest neighborhoods in the country. As I picked up the keys to the rental van, the missions leader gave me a sheet with some information about halfway houses on it. He said while I was in the Bronx, I should also make some stops to deliver Bibles to the halfway houses. I agreed to do so, loaded up the van with Bibles, and drove off to the Bronx by myself.

Once I pulled up to the police station, I noticed there was only one parking spot left by the front door. I was met in the parking lot by a female officer who asked me what I was doing. I shared that we got a call from a displeased police commander requesting me to come pick up some Bibles. I tried to park in the parking spot, and she told me "No, you can't park there. That's the commander's parking spot!"

Surprised at the circumstance, I asked her where I should park, and she told me there were no other spots. I told her I could be in and out quickly, so she said to go ahead and park in the commander's spot.

I entered the police station lobby and could not find the Bibles anywhere. An officer escorted me to the officer lounge, but there were no Bibles there either. Finally, when I walked back out into the lobby, another officer asked what I was trying to find. I told him about the Bibles, and he said, "Oh, we gave those out to all the officers this morning at roll call." Praise God, I thought! I exited the building and saw the female officer again. She stopped multiple lanes of traffic so I could back up the van and exit the station.

*I learned that God has a plan for us as we surrender to His will.*

I proceeded to the halfway houses to deliver Bibles and was met with folks glad to receive them. I had a few cases left over so I asked if there were any other nearby halfway houses. One resident said, "Don't you know where you are? There are drug addicts and halfway houses all over the place. Go down the block and make a left and you will see two more halfway houses." I left and followed his instructions. I found one halfway house but there was no parking. I double parked the van, put the hazard blinkers on, and quickly ran inside.

I walked up a flight of stairs and met a desk attendant. The attendant shared that they had fifty-six rooms, which meant I would need to carry three cases of Bibles. I ran back outside and walked down the front stoop, where a man was talking on his cell phone. I knew I would need to get the Bibles delivered quickly before I got a parking ticket.

At that moment God gave me a boldness to tap on the man's elbow and interrupt his phone call. He turned around and looked at me puzzled. I shared that I needed some help, and he ended his phone call and began to follow me. We unloaded the three cases of Bibles and began to walk back to the halfway house. He asked me what I was doing, so I told him I was delivering Bibles for the residents of the halfway house. He said, "I live here, can I have one?" I said, "But of course you can."

It was at that very moment that I experienced something amazing. Time began to slow down, and all the peripheral distractions of sights and sounds began to fade away. I heard God whisper, "This is your divine appointment." I looked at the man in his eyes and asked him his name. He shared that it was Andrew. I said "Andrew, God forbid if something were to happen to you today, do you know if you would go to heaven?" He responded that he hoped so because he was trying to turn his life around and quit drugs. Then I shared the Good News, that Jesus died on the cross for our sins so we could be forgiven and saved.

I told him that one of the last things recorded that Jesus said on the cross was "It is finished." I told Andrew that when it comes to salvation, we cannot earn it, nor do we deserve it. It is a gift of God's grace through faith in the completed work of Jesus dying on the cross as the ultimate sacrifice for our forgiveness.

After sharing the Gospel, Andrew responded by praying right there on the sidewalk to receive Jesus as his Savior. He looked at me after experiencing the peace of God and said, "I feel so much better. This means so much more than you know." I felt like I went back to the van and drove away floating from that experience.

God may have sent me all the way to New York City to stand on a sidewalk in front a man named Andrew in the Bronx so he could be saved by God's grace. I praise God for answering the prayer that morning in the hotel for surrendering my will for God's will. I thought I was going on a mission to ease over a mad police commander, and God used that situation to reroute me for His purposes. Hallelujah!

On another occasion I was on a mission trip in Orlando, Florida. It was quite hot and humid, and one day I found myself driving a large rental truck with thousands of Bibles in the back. I was responsible for delivering these Bibles to hotels all throughout International Drive, which is close to the world-renowned theme parks, like Disney World and Universal Studios.

I had about seven stops to make that day to hotels of various sizes. During the early afternoon, I had reached my fifth stop of the day, which happened to be at the largest hotel on the list. This hotel was so massive, it was split into two building towers and had a total of 1,641 rooms. That is a lot of rooms to fill with Bibles! Delivering to a hotel that size meant I would have to drive behind the building and back the truck up to a loading dock. After asking an employee of the hotel where to go, I drove around the hotel and backed the truck up to the dock.

I had another man helping me, so after we lifted the back gate of the truck, we maneuvered a pallet jack to lift one pallet. Dropping off 1,641 Bibles meant it would take a pallet and a half full of Bibles. The pallet lifted on the jack and we began to try to push the pallet forward. As it turned out, the truck was backed up on a reverse incline, meaning we were trying to push the pallet upwards out of the truck.

At about a pound per Bible, the first pallet weighed around 1,200 pounds. I am not a physics expert, but two guys each weighing under 200 pounds trying to push 1,200 pounds on an upward incline did not work well. We pushed and pushed to no avail.

Finally, feeling frustrated, we called our contact at the hotel requesting help. He shared that the employee working at the loading dock who was authorized to drive the forklift had already left for the day. Feeling discouraged, I began to lose hope in our ability to deliver the Bibles.

Another hotel employee happened to be present at the loading dock and observed our frustration. He approached us and began a conversation with us. He told us he was from Haiti. He then began to talk at length about the problems with the current affairs in his home country. He spoke of corruption among other things. The more he talked, the more frustrated I became as I thought about the remaining stops we had left on our list.

It was at that moment of frustration that I felt God speak softly to me a simple phrase. He said, "Look at him in the eyes." Therefore, I looked at the man in his eyes. He continued to ramble about Haiti, and I continued to look at him in his eyes. Then I felt another prompting from the Lord, "I want you to minister to him."

I looked down in the truck and saw an opened box of Bibles. I grabbed one and walked over toward him. I was kneeling on the truck looking down at the man who was standing below. I asked him his name and he replied, "Macendy." I greeted him and said I had a gift for him, God's Word. He responded, "Yes, I am familiar with the Bible. My parents took me to church when I was a child in Haiti." I said, "That's great. God forbid, if something were to happen to you today, are you confident you would go to heaven?" His eyes flinched away for a moment, signifying his uncertainty. That was all the answer I needed.

I began to share the Good News with Macendy and encouraged him that surrendering his life to the Lord was the best thing he could ever do. I asked him if he was ready, and he replied, "yes." We then bowed our heads as Macendy began to earnestly pray to receive Jesus as his Savior. Once again, I felt like I was floating after experiencing the presence of God moving amid the situation!

At that moment, I turned around and was reminded of our predicament. As Macendy was walking away, I had a thought and then shouted "Hey Macendy, what if we were to pull the truck off this incline and park it sideways to unload the Bibles; would that be okay?" He said "Yes, hold on and I will get some help."

Before I knew it, four of us, including Macendy, were unloading the 1,641 Bibles from the truck to make the delivery. God had blessed my obedience with the results. There I was thinking this man was a distraction, when really, he was a divine appointment!

*I simply had to release my agenda for God's agenda.*

One time I conducted an evangelism training event and then paired people in twos to go out and share Christ on the streets of downtown Albany, Georgia. After everyone was paired up, I was the last one left. Although I was not paired up with anyone, I prayed that God would lead me where to go. I grabbed a stack of Bibles and began to walk out of the hotel.

To my surprise, I bumped into a friend in the hotel lobby with whom I had served on a recent mission trip in New York City. His name was Jose, and he spoke little English. I remembered going into Spanish Harlem in New York City six months earlier not knowing how I would minister to people on the streets there who spoke Spanish, and God used Jose to help with that very thing while we were there. Again, you can imagine my surprise to see him. He was excited to join me in more street evangelism, this time in southern Georgia.

After prayer, we went out onto the streets and God blessed us with so many opportunities to share the Gospel and pray with people. I can remember being down to my last two Bibles. We noticed two guys standing on a street corner in front of the downtown library. We approached them and began to share the Good News. It turned out that they were both pastors of local churches. They were greatly encouraged to see what we were doing and prayed for us.

Then we walked back toward my car. As we were walking, God made it clear for us to stop and talk with a woman on the sidewalk. She was a bit older and very skinny. I told her that we were out ministering to people and asked if we could pray for her. I was quite surprised by her response.

She shared that her name was Melissa, and that she was diagnosed with stage four cancer. Her doctor had just informed her that she only had a few months to live. In that moment, God gave me a boldness and the words just flowed out. I looked at her in the eyes and said, "Melissa, I'm terminal, Jose is terminal, we are all terminal. There will be a point in time when our life ends, and we approach the judgment seat of God. The only way into heaven is what happens in our life with Christ."

I asked her if she was born again. She said she did not think so. I then shared the Gospel message, that Jesus proclaimed, "It is finished," and that to be saved, we must be born again. I told her that when she receives Jesus as her Savior, God's Spirit comes in and she can be a born-again child of God. I asked Melissa if she wanted to receive Christ and she said, "yes." We all then bowed our heads as Melissa prayed to receive Jesus as her Savior to become born again. She started to weep right there on the sidewalk.

I asked her what she was experiencing. She said as she was praying, it felt as if all her pain was melting. She was experiencing the peace of God! I then told her that people would want to know where she was getting that peace amid a dire situation, and now she could tell them it came from Jesus. I encouraged her that God still had a plan for her life, and she could point many to Christ.

I walked away so humbled and thankful for God's divine appointment with Melissa. I thought about the sense of urgency I needed to have for anyone God would allow me to share Christ with. I had thought we were finished, and as I was prepared to head back to the hotel, God revealed His agenda over mine!

Sometimes releasing our agenda and yielding to God's agenda presses us even at what can seem to be inopportune times. For years, I have been blessed to serve as a volunteer chaplain at the largest homeless shelter in my hometown. Typically, around 300 men sleep in this shelter on a nightly basis. All of them are required to attend an evening chapel service before bedding down.

Many times, I have been invited to preach at these chapel services and I always ask God to give me the words to say. One time, as I was sitting on the pew holding a Bible and praying for God to show me where in His Word to preach from, I did not seem to get clarity. After the opening worship songs, I got up to deliver the message.

As I approached the podium, I opened the Bible and set it down in front of me. At that point I felt compelled to simply start calling out the names of God in adoration and praise. I looked out at the crowd and began speaking, saying "He is the first and the last, the Alpha and the Omega, the chief cornerstone, the rock of our salvation."

I continued in praise, and before I knew it, I saw a wave of worship to the Lord erupt throughout the assembly of homeless men. There was clapping and shouting of praises. It was so humbling and overwhelming. God was taking over without me having to prepare. His presence was our gift as we honored Him! Hallelujah!!

What freedom and joy we can experience when we surrender all unto Him. We just need to be willing and available. Once I heard it said that God is looking less at our ability, and more at our availability. I believe He wants us to always be ready and willing to share the Good News with others. In 2 Timothy 4:2, we read:

"...preach the word; be ready in season and out of season;"

God opened a door for me to enter Folsom State Prison in northern California. I was blessed to enter the prison alone. I waited to meet the chaplain, and he escorted me through the prison to an open yard. We walked through the yard full of hundreds of inmates toward his office. Sometime later, I went back out onto the yard and began to speak with inmates.

Near the gate was a tall man. We began to talk, and he said he needed prayer. Upon discussion, he shared that he was unsure of his salvation. In that very moment and without any preparation, God allowed me to articulate the Gospel to him. He responded and we prayed for him to be saved. What an unexpected opportunity to share the Word of God!

One day I was on a college campus in Atlanta, Georgia distributing Bibles to students. I was in a high foot-traffic area near the student union building. Many students were walking by, and I had opportunities to give out many Bibles. In the busyness of the foot traffic, a young student from India came walking by. I offered her a Bible, and she accepted it. It was in that moment that I felt the Lord whisper to me, "Slow down."

I became mindful to just slow down and began a conversation with her. She shared that her name was Cushy. I shared the Gospel with her, and within moments she prayed to receive Jesus. It was a beautiful reminder of the simplicity of sharing the Gospel and not overcomplicating it. Praise God for unexpected moments to share the Word, and for His grace in helping me to slow down.

One day after leading another street evangelism training in New York City, I took a group with me to Rockefeller Center in Manhattan. We fanned out two by two and began to look for opportunities to tell people about Jesus. After a while, I decided to take a break and headed toward the open common area with flags of nations from all over the world. This is a famous area of the city.

As I was standing there, the Lord prompted me to speak with a man standing next to me. He was from Asia and was only on a short visit to America. I offered him a Bible, and he accepted it. I then shared the Gospel with him, and we prayed together for him to receive Christ. He expressed gratitude for the Bible and said he wanted to read it. There I was, thinking I was at a random spot to take a break, and God was setting up a divine appointment!

*As the Scripture reminds us, we need to be ready "in and out of season."*

# Chapter 8

## *The Power of Prayer*

Early on, as I read through the Bible, I was amazed at the many instances where signs and wonders occurred, especially in the New Testament. The Book of Acts was incredibly insightful as the disciples were experiencing God move mightily in and through them. I began to pray and ask God to take me to a deeper level of understanding faith, prayer, and experiencing His power in a more personal and profound way. I would pray specifically that He might show me more firsthand encounters of the power of His deliverance and healing.

Let me pause here to share that God is fully capable of anything. He is the sovereign God, the creator and sustainer of heaven and earth and everything in it. Sometimes we do not understand why He answers prayer for healing or deliverance in different ways and at different times. Sometimes He chooses not to heal people in the way we might desire or in the timing we expect it.

However, we can trust that His will is good, and that ultimately, He is mighty to save, heal, and deliver. It is a blessing that He allows us to pray by faith and trust Him for the results. Praying by faith is outlined in James 5:13-18, which reads:

> "Is anyone among you suffering? Let him pray. Is anyone cheerful? Let him sing praise. [14] Is anyone among you sick? Let him call for the elders of the church, and let them pray over him, anointing him with oil in the name of the Lord. [15] And the prayer of faith will save the one who is sick, and the Lord will raise him up. And if he has committed sins, he will be forgiven. [16] Therefore, confess your sins to one another and pray for one another, that you may be healed. The prayer of a righteous person has great power as it is working. [17] Elijah was a man with a nature like ours, and he prayed fervently that it might not rain, and for three years and six months it did not rain on the earth. [18] Then he prayed again, and heaven gave rain, and the earth bore its fruit."

Spiritual warfare is real. There is a war going on for souls. People can be oppressed and even possessed by demonic forces. As I mentioned before, I had begun to pray for God to take me into a deeper understanding of these things.

Around that time, I experienced an instance where a friend of mine had a demonic attack. He began to go house to house, telling people that he was Jesus Christ of Nazareth, and the evil spirit even led him to stand in the middle of an intersection of traffic. The police were called, and he was escorted to a local hospital where they sedated him, unconscious.

When I heard about what happened, I began to pray fervently and then went to visit him in the hospital. As I was on the way, a lady prayer warrior called me and began to pray over me. This has happened several times with her. She would call me during instances where I would need much prayer support, which was another reminder of God's sufficiency and grace. He always knows all things.

When I got to the hospital, I was told that he was in the emergency room. I went in and saw that he was heavily sedated and that he had a catheter. I could hear his heart beating through the monitor in the room. As I sat near him, a nurse was also monitoring him, so I just began to pray silently. I began to pray earnestly for deliverance.

His heart rate started increasing out of nowhere, and the beeping on the machine began going at a faster rate of speed. Suddenly I noticed that his catheter was filling. The nurse stood up, got nervous, and said "You are going to have to leave." She did not understand what was going on, but immediately I knew that it was spiritual warfare. I began to continue praying.

Before I went back to visit with him, I spoke with several people that knew him and many people had begun fasting and praying over him. I began to break down in tears as the Lord had given me such a burden for him. I would pray and pray and pray, and the tears would be streaming out as I just wanted so badly for him to be delivered.

The next night, I went to revisit him at the hospital. At that point, he had been admitted into a room. He was awake, but his tongue was fully swollen, and he could hardly speak. As he tried to talk, it sounded as if he had a gag reflex, so I just knelt by his bed on the floor and continued to pray for deliverance. Suddenly out of nowhere his tongue reduced back down to size and he stood up on the bed with his hands in the air as he said, "I can feel God's presence! I can feel God's presence! Raise your hands, raise your hands, raise your hands, Reza. Put your hands up and worship God with me!"

I put my hands up and began to praise the Lord, and it was as if the presence of God was swirling in that hospital room as my friend was magnificently delivered from that demonic spirit. He said, "I'm free, I'm free. I'm ready to go now; I'm ready to go!" With a smile on my face, I said, "Brother, I don't think they're going to let you go right now."

The doctors had inevitably thought that he had some type of psychiatric problem, and I knew it was going to be a while before he could leave. However, I said, "It's going to be at least tomorrow before you can get out of here." He said, "How long would that be?" I told him, "I don't know, maybe about ten more hours." He said, "No problem! That is ten more hours I can praise the Lord! Praise the Lord! Praise the Lord!"

He had his hands up just praising God, bouncing on the hospital bed. It was the most amazing sight to see such a close encounter of someone delivered from a spiritual attack in an obvious, transparent, and amazing way. Even as I write this, it seems hard to believe. Glory to God!

There was another instance I experienced in a different hospital. A friend of mine and I were going out to eat dinner, and before we went, she said to me, "Hey, let's go and stop by this hospital to see some friends of mine." I said, "No problem," and so we went.

As I walked into the hospital room door, my heart melted as I saw a little 3-year-old girl in what appeared to be a coma. I noticed that she was completely unconscious, that there were many machines attached to her, and her family was there. I became aware that her kidneys were failing her, so she was not conscious and completely pale.

I remember thinking immediately that God could heal her. I saw that everyone was trusting in these machines, but that God could ultimately heal her, and so I began to pray. Before we left, I went to the bathroom and as I was washing my hands, I asked God if He might allow me to lay hands upon her and pray for her healing. I went back into the hospital room, and before we left, I asked permission from the parents if I could pray over her. They said, "Of course."

I went over to her, looked at her, laid my hands on her arm, and said, "In the name of Jesus be healed." Then we all surrounded her and began to pray. Everyone in the room was holding hands. My left hand was on her arm, and my right hand held my friend's hand. She held hands with the girl's father, who was holding hands with the little girl's mother. On the other side, her mother held the other hand of the little girl on the bed, so that we were completely surrounding her.

We all prayed genuinely for her healing. Her parents were crying. As I walked out of that hospital room after the prayer, I was in the hallway, and the presence of God fell on me so strong that I almost collapsed and felt overwhelmed with emotion. I tried my best to hold my composure because there was a nurse right there in the hallway.

When we got down to the lobby of the hospital, I told the little girl's father, "Hey, I want to let you know that she is going to be okay—that God is going to take care of her." He said, "Yes, I know. We have people that are praying for her all over the world." I said, "Yeah, but I just want to make sure you know God spoke to me tonight and that your little girl is going to be okay."

That was on a Saturday evening. Within a few days, I received a phone call from her father. I missed the call, so it went to the voicemail, and he said something like, "Reza, Reza, you're not going to believe this. The doctor doesn't understand how, but her kidneys are working and she's out of the coma. She's healed!" I replied to him the Scripture verse in Mark 16 where it says, "These signs shall follow those who believe, they shall lay hands on the sick and they shall be healed..." and I knew instantly that God had healed her beyond any scientific or medical explanation.

My friend later told me that her grandmother came to faith in the Lord or that her faith was strengthened though that process. As a result, maybe God had brought about the whole situation to bring the family closer to Him. It was an amazing sign and wonder. Glory to God!

Years later, God blessed me with another instance of His healing power. Over time, I had the joy of conducting a lot of street ministry, mainly concentrating on ministering to homeless populations in the downtown areas of many cities like Charlotte, North Carolina, Nashville, Tennessee, and Los Angeles, California. One day I was in downtown Nashville, ministering to the homeless in a lot in which many homeless people would often congregate. I was there with a few others, and we had a few vehicles parked at the corner of the lot with free items including snacks, clothes, water, toiletries, and Bibles.

I was walking down the block, encouraging the homeless men and women to go over to the vehicles to get some needed supplies. One man was sitting on the ground, and I encouraged him the same. He was only about a half-block from the vehicles. He responded by saying it was too far for him to go. I said, "Look, it's just a half-block away." He said that I did not understand. He described his foot being in pain for weeks, and he literally could not walk on it.

I encouraged him to try so someone could pray for his healing. He looked up at me and said, "I believe God would hear your prayers." I was immediately convicted and knelt next to him. I looked at my hands, palms up, and began to pray that God would move mightily. I then laid my hands on his feet and prayed for healing in the name of Jesus. The man jumped up and began to praise God.

I was surprised and asked him what happened. He described a popping sensation in his foot during the prayer and was able to get up immediately. He again reminded me that he was genuinely unable to walk for three weeks straight, but now he could walk. I walked with him over to the vehicles where he received the supplies. God had answered prayer in an immediate, miraculous way!

Years ago, I was invited to help deliver a dignitary Bible to the Commissioner of the Georgia Department of Corrections. It was to occur during a luncheon where I was also given a few minutes to share about the impact of prison ministry. Early that morning, around 2:30 a.m., I felt the Lord awaken me to enter a time of prayer. I began to pray but did not know how. Therefore, I simply asked God to reveal to me prayer needs. He prompted me to pray that He would move on the heart of those in authority.

Not completely understanding why, I agreed and began to pray fervently that He would move on the heart of those in authority. I prayed for a while and then tried to go back to sleep but could not. I kept praying and trying to sleep but remained awake. I wrestled through that prayer for hours, almost until 5:30 a.m.

That day I went to the luncheon, and the dignitary Bible was presented to the Commissioner. Many of the GDOC staff were there as well. Then, I got up and shared stories of how God was moving even in maximum-security prisons and violent prison yards. I shared examples of experiences I had in prisons in Tennessee, California, and Louisiana. I felt the Lord give me the wisdom to share highlights, even in terms that resonated with the prison officials. I cited not only the power of God's salvation, but also how lives were being changed, and assault rates were decreasing— with less violence on the prison yards and in cell blocks as a result of ministry efforts. I sat down for the rest of the luncheon.

Afterward, a big man came walking up to me and shook my hand very firmly. He introduced himself as the Associate Commissioner of Operations for the entire state of the Georgia Department of Corrections. He looked at me in the eyes and said, "I heard what you said, and we need that here in Georgia. I'm going to give you guys access to all the prisons in Georgia." A bit stunned, I said, "Okay." He then said, "I don't think you understand. We have thirty-three prisons in the state of Georgia, and I am over all the wardens. When I say something is going to happen, it does." I replied, "Yes, sir."

On the way out the door, the Director of Chaplains grabbed me and asked if I could spare a few minutes to meet him in his office; I agreed. We sat down and he said, "I don't think you understand what just happened. In Georgia we have thirty-three state prisons, but eleven of them are known as Tier Two Prisons. That means they are maximum-security with twenty-three hours-a-day inmate lockdown. I have been trying to get volunteer access into these prisons for years with no avail. God just now moved on that man's heart, and now we have access to all of them."

I was even more stunned, and as I drove home, tears were running down my face. I realized God had clearly and directly answered my prayer. He moved on the heart of those in authority. But even more so, He shared a glimpse of His love for those inmates. In the years to follow, I helped launch new ministries in those eleven Tier Two maximum-security prisons, where volunteers go cell to cell to bring the Good News to the inmates. Over 600 of those prison inmates have since prayed to receive Jesus as their Savior, glory to God!

A similar experience happened another time where I was scheduled to speak. It was a much larger event, where thousands of people came from all over the world to be challenged and inspired in their ministry work. At the end of the session, I was preparing to give a brief challenge to the crowd to go out and share the Gospel on the streets.

Early in the morning on the day I was scheduled to speak, the Lord awoke me, and I began to pray. I prayed for the attendees and prayed that God would give me words to say. Then, I felt the Lord tell me that the people were not sharing their faith with others during the event as He wanted them to. I began to think, "How is it that I can stand on a stage and tell all these people that the Lord wanted them to more actively share their faith with others?"

I prayed and trusted the Lord. When the time came, God gave me a sense of peace as I walked onto the stage. I told them God awoke me and put a word on my heart. I told them not to let cultural barriers, or the fear of others' perceptions of them, get in the way of doing what God was calling them to do.

After the message, I received reports from individuals who said they were indeed afraid and were not going to share the Gospel. After being convicted by the message, they pressed on and did it by faith. As a result, they were used by God, and people out on the streets came to Christ that day. Glory to God!

Recently, I was back in New York City on another mission trip. The purpose of the trip was to share Christ with many people on the streets of Manhattan and help distribute hundreds of thousands of Bibles throughout the entire city. I was asked to help lead an evangelism training session for two days in a row—and lead teams out on the streets to evangelize immediately after each training session. These sessions happened back-to-back on a Saturday and Sunday.

During the session on Saturday, I felt prompted to challenge the group to ask God to show them people through His eyes; to be open to sharing the Gospel with whomever they came across regardless of age, race, or economic status. After the training, we went to lower Manhattan to an area called Battery Park. It was a beautiful day, and we split up two by two, ministering to people in the park. We could see the Statue of Liberty off in the distance in the background.

God opened many doors, and I was blessed to pray with many people that day. As we were finishing up, a few of the people I was with wanted to see the World Trade Center memorial, so we began to walk a few blocks north. In doing so, we passed through the area of Wall Street. As we were walking down the sidewalk, I heard a noise to my right and looked over. A homeless man was settling down for the night in the window of a bank. I thought to myself how ironic it was to see a homeless man sleeping in the window of a multimillion-dollar bank building near one of the world's wealthiest areas. We continued walking toward our destination, eventually had dinner, and traveled back to the hotel.

That evening, I awoke early in the morning with a deep burden for prayer. It was around 3:00 a.m. and the first image I saw in my mind was that homeless man in the window. I began to pray earnestly for him. Then I began to pray for the homeless population throughout the city. The thought came to my mind, "Who am I to have this nice comfortable hotel bed to sleep on while so many others are outside sleeping in windows, on sidewalks, and public benches?" I felt a conviction and a burden for the homeless. The prayer time went on several hours that evening, almost until dawn.

That day, I spoke at a nearby church and then conducted another street evangelism training that afternoon. Afterward, we went out onto the streets of Manhattan. As I was walking toward Times Square, we were only a few blocks away when I felt like God illuminated a lady sitting on the edge of the sidewalk next to a tall building. She was a middle-aged woman with about four large bags near her and a little dog on her lap as hordes of people were walking by her. I knew right away she was homeless. It was as if the Lord gave me an immediate prompting: *"her."*

I made my way through the crowd to her and knelt next to her. With a big smile on my face, I simply shared that I wanted to bless her with a gift of God's Word and offer her prayer. I told her my name, and she shared her name was Leah. Then God began to give me words to say to her. I shared that God loved her and had a plan for her life. Then I shared the Gospel message, that God had sent His Son Jesus to die for her on a cross so she could be forgiven of her sins.

I told her that nobody is perfect, and that we all need forgiveness. She listened intently. I asked her if she was ready to receive that forgiveness by accepting Jesus as her personal Savior. She looked up and said, "yes." At that moment, Leah prayed to receive Christ as her Savior right there on a busy sidewalk near Times Square.

It was marvelous! But then something else miraculous happened. At that very moment, as all those people were passing by, a lady stopped and looked over. After the prayer, she shouted through the crowd of passersby, "Did she just receive Jesus Christ?"

Stunned by the unexpected question, I looked up and said, "yes." Then the lady made her way through the crowd and began to talk with Leah. The lady shared that she was wealthy, living in New York, and many people judged her for that. Then she said, "What most people don't know is that I'm from Germany, and back in Berlin, I was homeless. At that point, I gave my life to Jesus Christ, and He saved me and got me off the streets. Did you just now receive Jesus Christ for the first time?"

Leah said yes. Then the lady said, "Good! Now you are a child of God, and He wants to pull you off these streets too!" I could not believe it. Right at the moment when Leah received Christ, in the sovereignty of God, He sent a lady to immediately witness to her in a way that I never could. Hallelujah!

Considering the complete sovereignty of God, I was blessed to experience something unique. I was in Chicago for a mission trip to evangelize in the city. On the first day, I went out with a group to distribute Bibles to students at several high schools. Early in the morning, we found out that there would be severe storms rolling through the area. We began to pray and ask God to reroute the rain so we could successfully reach the students. As we looked at the radar, the line of storms was so severe that another team scheduled to go out the same day decided to cancel.

My team went out anyway and targeted some of the most challenging schools in South Chicago. Police officers are stationed at these schools because it is prevalent for fights to erupt among the students upon dismissal. In fact, at one school we visited, a fight did erupt, and surprisingly the officers just watched as it was such a common occurrence.

We were blessed to provide almost every student with God's Word that day. Somehow the weather was holding out, and we did not experience much rain. I looked at the Doppler radar on an app on my phone and was stunned to see that the storm broke up and missed our part of town. As we distributed the final few Bibles to students, the rain began to pick up. I had experienced a miraculous answer to prayer as God sheltered us from a massive rainstorm to accomplish His will that day!

*I learned that we should always recognize the incredible gift of freely petitioning God in prayer.*

# Chapter 9

## *The Power of Intercessory Prayer*

There have been many exciting instances when the Lord clearly directed me how to pray, and He has also shown me the answers to those prayers in real-time. In Ephesians 6:18, we read:

> "...praying at all times in the Spirit, with all prayer and supplication."

I remember early on as I was actively involved in a local jail ministry, I would go every Monday evening to the county jail and minister to the inmates. Week after week, I would go with a few other volunteers, and God would bless us immensely. After an officer's announcement, inmates would come out of their cell pods into a small classroom for a Bible study.

One Monday, when I was on the way to the jail, I began to pray for the inmates. I prayed something like, "God, I don't know what to say to the inmates tonight, so please help me honor You by sharing what You want me to." At that moment, as I was driving, it seemed like I saw a flash of white letters right in front of me on the windshield. It happened so fast. The letters read, "WITCHCRAFT." I was both stunned and intimidated by how to bring it up during my time with the inmates.

That evening, around a dozen inmates came into the room, and we had a great time of fellowship, reading from the Word, and having group prayer. However, throughout the evening, I knew I was prompted to bring up witchcraft but felt too intimidated. I missed the opportunity and went home. That night, I prayed that God would forgive me for my disobedience and that I would be bolder in the future.

The next Monday came around, and I went back to the jail. This time, the other volunteers were unavailable. I prayed as I waited for the inmates to enter the room with me. To my surprise, only one inmate came in that night. We greeted each other and sat down to begin our discussion.

With my disobedience still convicting me from the week before, I decided to blurt it out. I told him that God gave me a word the week before, but I was too afraid to bring it up. He eagerly looked at me to share it with him as I was speaking...and soon enough, I said, "and that word was, 'witchcraft.'" As soon as I said the word, "witchcraft," his head dropped, and he cracked a smile. He said, "It's funny you should mention that, because I am the only one in this jail that knows anything about it."

He shared that he was from New Orleans and practiced black magic in the jail that he had learned from his hometown. I said, "Okay, let's see what God's Word says about that." We read together Scripture verses in the book of Galatians that those who practice witchcraft would not inherit the Kingdom of God. At the end of our study, we prayed together for him to repent.

I was in awe of how God used even my disobedience to move in my life and give me a second chance to honor Him. He even held all the other inmates back to redeem the time with exactly who He wanted me to minister to in these moments!

*It all started with a prayer to align my service with God's plan.*

A similar thing happened another time when I was traveling to Pensacola for a mission trip. God had opened the door for me to speak at a homeless shelter there called the Waterfront Rescue Mission. As I was traveling to Pensacola, I began to pray and ask God for guidance in my message.

I openly confessed that I did not want to give a message that I thought was good, but I wanted it to be from God. Through the prayer, God directed me to Psalm 51, where David pens a Psalm of repentance. One of the critical verses was, "Create in me a clean heart." It is all about seeking God's forgiveness and saving grace.

During the night of the event, I spoke at length, walking the homeless men in attendance through the entire Psalm. There must have been upwards of a hundred men in attendance. Afterward, I gave an invitation for men to come forward to receive prayer. Many of the men responded by coming forward and lined up for prayer.

I will never forget, finally getting to the last man in line. I asked him what I could pray for, and he said, "Just pray as you feel led." I agreed and began to pray for God's blessings over him. Just as I was praying, God impressed on me to pray for him to be delivered from suicide. I interrupted my prayer and began to pray out loud for this deliverance from suicide. The young man began to weep.

After the prayer, he looked at me and said something shocking. He said, "There is no way you could have known about that. Before this service, I was out in the woods nearby, with a pistol under my chin about to commit suicide. Something told me not to do it, so I came to the service here tonight."

He also shared that his father had committed suicide years before. Stunned, I looked at him and shared that God had great plans for his life, and we continued in prayer. Here I was standing in front of a young man who almost killed himself an hour earlier, being just a mere vessel of God's redeeming love toward him. He was right—there was no way I could have known that. But God knew. My job was to listen and pray.

94

God opened another door for me to enter one of the country's most notorious prisons, San Quentin State Prison, in northern California. I was excited about this opportunity as I had been praying about it for some time. The Lord blessed me to enter the prison on a one-time basis. As I approached the guard at the entrance, I was amazed at the prison building's old castle-like architecture. This also happens to be one of the oldest still-functioning prisons in the country, which opened back in 1852.

I went into an area called the Badger unit; a portion of the prison allocated for housing inmates who had recently arrived. As I entered the unit, it was noisy, and I noticed the long tiers of cells that were multiple stories high. There was a catwalk type platform in which an officer walked on with weapon in hand.

The inmates were housed in cells behind bars in sets of two. The row of cells stretched all the way down the tier. I began to go cell to cell, ministering to the inmates, distributing God's Word, and offering prayer. God blessed tremendously, providing many encounters with receptive inmates.

I can clearly remember one of the cells where two inmates were housed. As I looked at them through the bars, I offered prayer support. They agreed to receive prayer, and one inmate told me to just pray as I felt led. I agreed and then began to pray, seeking the Lord on how to pray for them. In the middle of the prayer, God gave me a word of knowledge and I began to intercede.

I prayed specifically for God to put a hedge of protection around these men, and precisely that He would deliver them from anxiety and "night terrors." That was an unusual phrase for me, but I prayed as I felt led and continued. I could sense God moving during the prayer.

Afterward, the inmates expressed great appreciation as they looked at each other and then me. In prison, it is hard for men to express weakness. The words were not said, but I could immediately tell that specific prayer was exactly needed for either or both men. Praise God for allowing us insight on how to pray specifically as we intercede for others!

Another time I was in the middle of a large pod of inmates in a maximum-security prison in Tennessee. God had told me to distribute His Word to all the inmates—and had opened an amazing door to do so. As I gave a Bible to an inmate in the middle of the pod, he asked if I could pray for him. I agreed and began to pray. In the middle of the prayer, God prompted me to stop, so I did.

I immediately paused and looked him in the eyes. I asked him if he was saved, and he responded that he was unsure. I shared the Gospel with him and asked if he was ready to receive Christ. He said, "yes," and then, right there, in the middle of a large pod of cells with hundreds of inmates around, we bowed our heads and prayed for him to receive Jesus. Praise God!

One time I was on a mission trip in Wisconsin and stayed with a dear couple. The husband was an evangelist that has been used all over the world to lead people to

Christ. During our time chatting, he shared an unusual thing that had been happening to him. He said that recently, whenever he would start sharing the Gospel with someone, suddenly, he would begin to feel nauseous and confused. Again, this only happened when he would share Christ. It became a daunting distraction to him when he was sharing his faith with others. I told him that I would certainly pray about that for him.

That evening, as I stayed in the guest room, I prayed God would alleviate this from the brother. That evening shortly after I fell asleep, I awoke with a clear vision to lay hands specifically on his temples and pray for deliverance. I immediately went downstairs and told him I believed God showed me how to pray for him. I asked him if I could lay hands and pray over him. He agreed, and we both knelt.

Just as I saw in the vision, I laid hands on both sides of his temples and prayed for deliverance in the name of Jesus. We both could sense the presence of God. Years later, the same man told me that since we prayed that evening, he never experienced the same symptoms while sharing the Gospel. What a unique experience, praise the Lord!

It is amazing what happens if we will listen to God. One day as I was ministering to the homeless in downtown Nashville, I approached a group sitting on a park bench. I would usually start the conversation by letting them know that I wanted to pray for them. I asked if there were any prayer requests. Nobody answered, and they seemed a bit disinterested.

I continued in prayer, asking God to lead the way. I felt the Lord prompt me to pray over someone's stomach. I asked if anyone sitting on the bench had any particular health needs, and that the Lord had just prompted me to pray for someone's stomach area. The man on the bench closest to me immediately responded, "Yes, I've got a pain in my stomach area. How did you know that?"

I responded that I did not know, but God did. I prayed for his healing in Jesus' name, and he immediately felt better. This caught the attention of the whole bench and another lady sitting on the ground, and many started sharing specific prayers. God was revealing to them that He was real and attentive to their needs in a special way. What a blessing!

Early on, as I continued to learn the power of intercessory prayer, God opened a unique opportunity for me. At the time, my sister was a college student, living in an apartment near a university with three other young women. My sister shared with me that one of her roommates was struggling with drug addiction, so she asked me to come speak with her. I prayerfully agreed and drove to her apartment. Right before I entered the front door, I felt the Lord compel me to stop and pray. Out on the front doorstep I began to fervently pray, and God took me into a profound time of prayer for deliverance for this young lady.

This type of prayer was not merely a prayer of requests before the Lord, but more of a deep prayer of spiritual warfare against the powers and principalities of wickedness holding this young lady in bondage. We read in Ephesians 6:12:

> "For we do not wrestle against flesh and blood, but against the rulers, against the authorities, against the cosmic powers over this present darkness, against the spiritual forces of evil in the heavenly places."

I sensed the presence of God moving through those prayers. I then knocked and entered the front door. My sister shared that her roommate was in the back bedroom. I proceeded to knock on the back-bedroom door, and she invited me in. She shared that she was addicted to heroin, and her voice sounded scratchy and tired. I shared my testimony with her, how I had cried out to God, and He answered my prayer and gave me a new life in Him.

She then shared with me how she was raped at the age of twelve, and soon afterward, at the same age, she began to use heroin. She was then nineteen years old, so she had been addicted for almost seven years. I shared the Good News with her—that God loved her, that He could heal her, and most importantly, He could save her. She responded by saying she tried everything else, so she was willing to give God a try. We then bowed our heads as she prayed to receive Jesus as her Savior, for God to save, heal, and deliver her from her addiction. It was a marvelous time of prayer!

Afterward, she shared even more that surprised me. She said, "You don't know how many people have tried to convince me to become a Christian, but I never would listen. Something just seemed so real about the way you shared, that I thought it might be true." She then offered a few more surprising things. She shared that she had been practicing witchcraft and was high up on the order of witches. I told her that God had so much more for her and that she needed to start reading His Word.

She also shared that her boyfriend had just overdosed on heroin the night before and felt having each other was the only reason to live. After his overdose, she thought she would go ahead and use as much heroin as possible because there was no longer any hope without her boyfriend. She stated that she had planned to overdose that very night!

At that very moment, God gave me a word for her. I told her that there would be a time when she would be tempted, but she could call out to the living God and He would help her in her time of need. The next day, her heroin dealer found out about her boyfriend's overdose and felt terrible. He showed up at her apartment and gave her a free large bag of heroin. She immediately cooked it up and filled a syringe with it. She inserted the syringe in her arm and pulled back on it. Seeing a few drops of blood enter the syringe, she knew she got a good vein.

It was at that very moment, when she was ready to press the heroin into her vein, she remembered what I said the night before. She looked up and called out to the living God for help. He immediately convicted her, and she yanked the syringe out of her arm and threw it away. She had an encounter with the living God!

The next week, I followed up with her every day. She shared that she did not feel well detoxing from the heroin, but that she had experienced much worse symptoms while detoxing in the past. God was giving her grace. She then went to a bookstore and bought a Bible and began to read the Word. God had performed a miracle in her life through a great deliverance. He indeed answers prayers of intercession!

Another morning, I woke up in a hotel room in Georgia. I started my morning with prayer and spending time in God's Word. He brought me to Isaiah 61:1, where we read:

> "The Spirit of the Lord God is upon me,
>     because the Lord has anointed me
> to bring good news to the poor;
>     he has sent me to bind up the brokenhearted,
> to proclaim liberty to the captives,
>     and the opening of the prison to those who are bound;"

I immediately knew that God was calling me to go into a prison that day. The hotel where I was staying was less than 45 minutes from the largest prison in Georgia. After my prayer time, I drove to the prison with anticipation of what God would do. I had no personal agenda and was a bit nervous walking in the front door.

The prison was named GDCP, which stands for Georgia Diagnostic and Classification Prison. Throughout the entire state, every offender was routed through this prison for classification, and either remained there, or then transferred to another prison. This prison also housed the death row inmates in the state.

I showed the officer at the entrance my volunteer badge and the door buzzed open. I walked the hall remaining in an attitude of prayer. I then proceeded to one of the housing units. It reminded me of San Quentin, as the set up was the same. There were two stories of a long corridor of cells housing inmates behind open bars.

As I walked down the corridor in prayer, there was a lot of inmate chatter echoing through the unit. Inmates also watched me, and several tried to get my attention through the commotion as I walked by. About halfway down the corridor of cells, I felt prompted to stop. I immediately looked to my left and saw an inmate standing in his cell up against the bars. I looked at him directly in the eyes and walked up to him. I knew it was a divine appointment.

As I approached him, I noticed he had tattoos all over his torso and on his face. Without him saying a single word to me, I approached him, looked at him in the eyes, and told him God had a great plan for his life. It was a straightforward and direct message. The next sentence I stated was, "However, it us up to you to surrender your life to Him...Are you ready?"

I was astounded at the boldness God gave me and had no idea how he would respond. He looked at me right back and said, "Yes." I shared with him that Jesus died for his sins and that receiving Christ was the first step. Moments later, both of us were praying together as he made the decision to receive Christ and surrender his life to God. It was incredible. Afterward, we talked for a while, and I left.

It also turned out that day that there were other local volunteers in the prison, sharing Christ with inmates on another tier block. I later joined them, and we had an incredible time ministering to inmates for hours that day. God had once again answered prayers of intercession and led the way.

*God is so faithful.*

*Grace Upon Grace*

# Chapter 10

## *Experiencing Unexpected Blessings Through Obedience*

God has a way of blessing His people as they follow Him in acts of obedience. It does not mean the path will always be easy, but He will allow us to experience more of Him through the process as we learn to trust Him for His will in our lives. In Ephesians 3:20, we read:

> "Now to him who is able to do far more abundantly than all that we ask or think, according to the power at work within us…"

By the grace of God, I have been inside the death row units of prisons in three states. One time the Lord blessed me with another life lesson in a death row unit in Louisiana. At Angola Prison, the Louisiana State Penitentiary, I was blessed with an open door to go down the cell block of the death row unit, ministering to inmates one at a time through their cell bars.

I walked up to one inmate, and we began to chat. Through our discussion, he looked at me in the eyes and said "I would do anything to have the headaches you have in your life. To hear a car horn again. To be able to go to a refrigerator and pick out what I want to eat. To take my shoes off and know what it feels like to walk barefoot on grass."

I absorbed every word he said. That night I tossed and turned thinking about what he said, over and over. I realized that there was so much in life that we can take for granted. Over the years, I held onto those words to remind me to be more thankful for my freedoms and God's provision. What a life lesson in so few words!

As I continue to reminisce on God's unexpected blessings, I am also reminded of another prison experience. I was blessed to help start a ministry at Valdosta State Prison, a Tier Two prison in Georgia. A group of volunteers and I started the day in prayer, and then entered the prison. Since this was a brand-new ministry, we began by meeting with the warden, the prison chaplain, and other key staff. Then, we proceeded into housing units where men were on lockdown twenty-three hours a day.

It was a blessed day as we visited hundreds of cells, sharing the Gospel, and praying with inmates. This went on for hours. At the very last cell I visited, I was blessed to share the Good News with a young inmate. He responded, and we prayed together for him to receive the Lord. Afterward, he requested a pen from an officer that was walking by. The officer gave it to him, and he signed his name in the back of the Bible, signifying that he had given his life to the Lord.

As this was happening, I could see him kneeling on the floor through a pie flap in the cell door. He handed back the pen to the officer. Then, at the very moment the officer went to lock the pie flap, the inmate looked up at me and said, "Thank you." Then the flap was closed, and I never saw him again.

It was one of the most humbling moments of my life as I felt so unworthy to be involved in God's redemptive work. That last image of the heartfelt appreciation from this inmate was burned into my memory. What an unexpected blessing and a truly marvelous end to a first day of this new ministry outreach! God is so good to us!

One year when I was in New York City, God put on my heart to deliver Bibles to a large homeless shelter in the heart of lower Manhattan called the Bowery Mission. They were serving hundreds, if not thousands, of the city's homeless population daily. I called the chaplain and arranged a time to bring the Bibles.

I drove to lower Manhattan and parked a rental van out in front of the building. With the hazard blinkers on, I went inside to share that I, along with a few other volunteers, had arrived to deliver Bibles. A few of the homeless shelter volunteers came out to the van, and we unloaded hundreds of Bibles. The chaplain asked us to place them in a storage closet upstairs in his office, so we began carrying them there.

After we were finished, the chaplain was so grateful and gave us an overview of their ministry. He shared that Billy Graham preached from the podium right there in the shelter. We then spent some time praying over the chaplain.

Afterward, I told the chaplain that if he ever needed a fill-in for an evening service to let me know. Then we took a quick tour of the facility. As we were getting ready to leave, the chaplain came running out to grab our attention. He looked at me and said, "You're not going to believe this, but the pastor that was scheduled to conduct the service tonight just called and said he couldn't make it." Stunned and excited, I told the chaplain that we would be honored to do the service.

So, less than an hour later, there I was staring at the eyes of a shelter full of homeless men in New York City, sharing the Good News of the Gospel. At the end of the message, I gave an invitation and we watched as men came forward to receive Christ and pray for deliverance from drug addictions. What an incredible blessing and honor!

Recently, I was blessed to enter the Escambia County Jail in Pensacola, Florida. The Lord had put it on my heart to stop by and visit the jail's chaplain. I had visited this jail several times before and had the honor of helping provide Bibles to all the inmates. This is a larger jail, which almost 30,000 inmates go through every year. I had not been there in several years, and since I was traveling through Florida on a trip, I decided to stop by. The chaplain warmly greeted me in the jail lobby and escorted me up to the chapel.

When I arrived at the chapel, I also was met by another chaplain, and they asked if we could all go out to lunch. I agreed. We looked at the clock and realized it was only 10:30 a.m., so we had about an hour before lunch time. I told them I was available to serve as needed, and they sent me to follow a volunteer who was distributing reading glasses to the inmates. I agreed, and we started to visit several pods of inmates. The volunteer, pushing a cart full of reading glasses, would enter the pod, speak with an officer, and then give out the glasses to inmates who had requested them.

The first stop we visited was a female pod. One lady came forward to receive her glasses. Afterward, I asked if we could pray for her and she agreed. She shared a personal prayer request and we gladly prayed for her. Later, we visited another pod full of female inmates and one of the chaplains happened to also be in the pod. As the volunteer gave out the glasses, the chaplain asked me if I would like to address the entire pod. I said, "yes," and began to pray. Then, the chaplain called the entire pod to attention and introduced me.

God opened the door for me to share my testimony and a clear presentation of the Gospel. The women were sitting on their bunk beds as they were lined up throughout the room. Many responded by bowing their heads in prayer to receive Christ and ask for an infilling of His presence. It was amazing!

Afterward, I continued to follow the volunteer to other pods. This time we were on another floor in a unit that had four pods of inmates. The volunteer requested permission from the officer to open the door, and then went in to call out the names of inmates who requested glasses.

After the glasses were given out, the volunteer looked at me and asked if I wanted to address the pod. I prayerfully agreed and stepped forward. God gave me boldness, and I called the whole pod to attention. Men were watching television, playing cards, and talking on telephones that were attached to a wall. I once again began to share my testimony and then the Gospel. The men listened, and I was astounded when several responded by praying to receive Christ.

I remember the last pod we went to where a similar situation occurred. The volunteer stepped into a foyer area to deliver glasses and then told the men there was a visitor. I then stepped up to share my testimony and deliver the Gospel. Right when I got to the point of offering an invitation to receive Christ, I was pulled back. At that moment, there were several inmates that needed to enter the pod. I patiently stepped aside and began to pray.

After a few minutes I stepped back out and told the men that if God spoke to them, they could respond by faith and surrender their lives to the Lord. I could not believe what I saw. The men stopped playing cards, stopped watching television, and others even came out of their cells. There were inmates lined up on the second level leaning on the guardrails. It was as if the whole pod full of men was responding with heads bowed in prayer. God was on the move! I had no idea what God was going to do through me that day.

*It is tremendously humbling to experience God's blessings as we are obedient to do His will.*

# Chapter 11

## *God is Sovereign*

It is awe-inspiring to consider that God is truly sovereign over all things. In Colossians 1:16-17, we read:

> "For by him all things were created, in heaven and on earth, visible and invisible, whether thrones or dominions or rulers or authorities—all things were created through him and for him. And he is before all things, and in him all things hold together."

In the fall of 2011, I had the opportunity to go to Las Vegas to share the Gospel and give out Bibles. This was one of the most memorable experiences of my life. I remember having a flight delay from Seattle down to

Las Vegas. I got into town about 1–1:30 a.m., finally got to sleep, was up at 5 a.m., and shortly after I found myself driving a large rental truck around the strip of Las Vegas. I was amazed at how God had given me such an opportunity to hand-deliver so many Bibles.

To better describe the situation, I found myself driving a twenty-four-foot truck with about 14,000 pounds of Bibles in the back. I had never driven such a large truck before, and here I was driving it around the main strip and worldwide tourist destination of Las Vegas, Nevada.

It was amazing to see God's provision and how He can guide and direct, opening doors. Along with a few other volunteers in the truck, I helped service some of the largest casinos and resorts with the Word of God. Some of these facilities in and of themselves were like small cities. One of the largest hotels had 7,000 rooms and 2,000 housekeepers. Can you imagine that?

At some of these more extensive facilities, we had to go underground to make the deliveries of Bibles. At one of them, I drove up to a long line of trucks. We sat in the truck for about an hour, not moving an inch. We just sat and sat, and we thought, "This is never going to happen." In front of us was a long line of trucks delivering beer and food and whatever else. As we sat there, we decided to do the only thing we could: pray.

Afterward, we jumped out of the truck and began to stretch our legs. I pulled out my cell phone and began to take some pictures. There was a security camera on one of the walls and a security officer quickly walked up to me. He said, "Sir, what are you doing? You can't take pictures here." I responded, "Oh, I'm sorry. No problem."

Evidently, it was a security threat, so I began to delete the pictures right in front of him. He said, "Who are you and who are you with?" I said, "I'm Reza, and I'm here to deliver some Bibles." He asked for my identification. I pulled out my license, and he saw my name. He then said in a concerned tone, "What did you say you were doing again?" After repeating my objective of delivering the Bibles, he sternly said, "I'm sorry, you're going to need to leave now."

As you can imagine, I was quite disappointed and disheartened because I thought of all those rooms in the hotel that would not have a Bible. I began to apologize to the Lord for my error and got back in the truck. Since the truck was so large, we could not make a U-turn and therefore had to pass all the other trucks ahead of us. When we got to the gate, we were met by the same security officer and another one. I saw them whispering to each other and thought the situation might get even worse.

One of the security officers approached me and said, "Sir, before we let you through, we will need to search your truck." I said, "Ok, no problem," and hopped out of the truck to walk around back. I was calm and confident because I knew exactly what we had in the truck.

When I went to open the latch on the back of the truck, I looked at the officers and their eyes were opened wide, not knowing what to expect. When I lifted the back gate, they immediately saw pallet after pallet of

Bibles. One looked at the other, and then they noticed we had a hand truck and there was an electric lift on the back of the truck. One officer said, "Since you have your own hand truck and lift gate, you can go unload them yourself."

I was in awe at what had just happened. It was as if God parted the sea of the long line of trucks so that we could move ahead of everyone to deliver the Bibles! When it comes to the Word of God, He has a way of making miracles happen. I believe it all started with the prayer we prayed as we were stuck in the back of the line of trucks.

*I learned that what I thought was going wrong, God was redeeming for His glory!*

While serving the Lord, there have been many instances of seeing Him move on someone's heart to accomplish His purposes. One day I found myself in the south Bronx staring up at a large hospital. The purpose of the visit was to distribute Bibles to the patients and doctors.

As we entered the hospital with an eagerness to give out Bibles, I remember speaking with one doctor. He shared with me that we were in the most impoverished neighborhood in the country and that ninety-nine percent could not pay their medical bills. He said this neighborhood had ninety-nine percent indigence. I realized the severity of the poverty in the area where crime, violence, and drug abuse were rampant. I felt even more honored to be bringing hope through the Word of God.

Throughout the visit, I was blessed to give out many Bibles. One doctor came walking down the hall in a white coat and I offered him a Bible. He quickly shrugged me off and said, "No, I don't need that." As he walked away, I watched as God stopped him in his tracks. He turned around, looked at me in the eyes, and said, "You, grab a stack of those and follow me."

Surprised at his request, I quickly grabbed a stack of Bibles and began to follow the doctor. As we walked, he escorted me through a set of double doors. On the doors was a sign in yellow with big letters reading "CAUTION -WARNING."

Unsure of where we were going, I continued to follow the doctor. Then, we went through another set of double doors, again with the same signage. Before I knew it, I found myself in a large waiting area in front of a group of people.

The doctor got everyone's attention and said a few words. Then he instructed me to give out Bibles to all the people. Almost everyone in that waiting area took a Bible. I was stunned at what happened. Then as I walked out of the room, I realized exactly what had just happened.

I was in the middle of the HIV/AIDS ward in the poorest neighborhood in the country. What an amazing example of how God pursues all people. In John chapter 3, we read:

> "[16]For God so loved the world, that he gave his only Son, that whoever believes in him should not perish but have eternal life. [17] For God did not send his Son into

the world to condemn the world, but in order that the world might be saved through him."

This was a small example of how when God said He so loved the world; He meant the whole world! Praise God for His incredible hand of sovereignty! He certainly can move on the heart of those in authority. This experience highlighted that for me, for sure.

One day I felt an unusual call from the Lord. There was a large music festival happening in my state that lasted for three days, called "Bonnaroo." I was spending time with the Lord in prayer, and as it came to mind, I heard Him say, "Feed my sheep." I said okay and packed a bag full of Bibles. I drove an hour or so to the festival and began to walk through the crowd sharing Christ with others. It was a blessing.

In fact, I began to return to this music festival every year, but over time, God started to provide people to come along with me to go into the crowd two-by-two. One year I invited the worship pastor from my church. He was a bit intimidated but agreed to go by faith.

The crowd at such an event can quickly appear non-receptive to the Gospel. However, I have learned repeatedly not to judge by appearance and instead trust God for fruit as He leads. We entered the festival and endured some spiritual warfare. The pastor had to go away to a place alone to pray.

Later, we continued to navigate the crowds, handing out many Bibles. Eventually, we sat down on the lawn to listen to some music. There was a heavily dense crowd in front of us as the people got closer to the stage. Out of the dense crowd came walking toward us a young man. Without us even saying anything to him, he began a conversation with us. We invited him to sit with us and had a great conversation.

God opened a door for us to share the Gospel, and he prayed to give his life to the Lord! Afterward, he was very encouraged and stunned at what happened. He began to experience the peace of God. He then got up and walked back toward the crowd.

Right before he went beyond our sight and disappeared into the crowd, he stopped, turned around, looked at us, and gave a thumbs up. The pastor and I were amazed that God had sent someone to us without us saying a word to him! God is sovereign and can connect those He chooses to each other by His will.

One day I received a phone call from a prison chaplain in California. He was calling to invite me to help with a yard event at a prison in central California. A yard event is a large-scale outreach to hundreds of inmates at once. Usually there is a stage and a microphone. He explained that they needed a keynote speaker for the event, so I told him I would pray about it.

After spending time in prayer, I felt prompted to move forward. I let the chaplain know that God was compelling me to move forward. He was excited, and I put it on my calendar. I was also excited and continued to pray. Months later, I traveled to California and then made my way to the prison for a training event the evening before the outreach on the prison yard.

I was quite surprised at what I found out. Many leaders were present at the training, including several chaplains and the lead correction officer for the yard. The officer began to explain the situation, and it was then that I realized the conditions.

As it turns out, over the past few decades, the United States had experienced an explosive growth in the population of people in prisons and jails. Within forty years, the number grew from a few hundred thousand to over two million. California happens to be the state with the highest population in the United States, and the highest population of incarcerated people. There are many prisons in the state, and many have violent offenders that are affiliated with gangs.

Many California prisons are older facilities, spanning a history of operating from the mid 1800's on. This prison I was about to enter, Salinas Valley State Prison, was a newer prison that was less than twenty years old. When it opened, the other older prisons saw an opportunity to begin transferring their worst inmates to this newer prison.

Salinas Valley State Prison, in effect, became the end of the line for the California Department of Corrections. The worst offenders were sent there. If this was not bad enough, after arriving at Salinas Valley, the most violent and gang affiliated inmates were housed on a single yard together.

There were four yards in the prison; A, B, C, and D. The most violent and gang affiliated inmates were all housed in C yard. This in effect became one of the most violent prison yards in the entire country. It was reported that 1,500 violent acts occurred on that one yard in a single year.

At the training session the evening before the yard event, I found out that C yard would be the yard we were going on. The corrections officer shared with all the outreach volunteers the situation. In addition to the statistics, he also shared that there had not been an outreach on that yard in fourteen years. The last time they tried to do an outreach there an inmate was stabbed.

An average of four violent acts occurred on C yard every day. In preparing us, the officer said it was not a question of if, but when, a violent action would occur on C yard. He instructed us to back up toward the prison wall as officers would shoot down live ammunition on the yard, and he did not want us to get shot. He also shared that we would need to pay attention to which way the wind was blowing because the officers would also throw out tear gas, and he did not want us to be affected by it.

I thought, "Lord, is this where you are sending me?" He prompted me to go, and so all night, I entered fervent prayer. I knew that it would be a dangerous event, but that ultimately my life was in God's hands.

*When I surrendered all aspects of my emotions to God, He gave me a wonderful peace.*

The next day as I was getting ready to go out on the yard, two ladies approached me and said they felt led to pray for me. I agreed, and they began to fervently pray over me. After their prayers, one of the ladies told me that she saw a vision during the prayer time. She said she saw me in the vision shooting up arrows into the sky representing the Word of God, and that those arrows were going to land on certain inmates and penetrate their hearts. I had a renewed sense of confidence as I entered the prison.

A team of volunteers and I were blessed to conduct two outreaches on C yard that day: once in the morning and once in the afternoon. Each outreach lasted for approximately two hours and included worship music and a keynote message. I was blessed to deliver both keynote messages through a microphone and loudspeakers. It felt as if the Gospel message was reverberating off those prison walls covered by barbed wire!

Before the outreaches began, inmates began pouring out of the buildings onto the yard by the hundreds. They began to segregate themselves by race and gang, into four main groups. There were invisible boundaries in the yard where the inmates segregated themselves. As volunteers, we were entering into their territory. All eyes were on us as they poured out onto the yard.

The Lord blessed tremendously as the Word went forth, and many inmates came forward for prayer and further conversation with the volunteers. I felt as if God gave me an incredible boldness to proclaim His Word! I was physically exhausted but spiritually full. It felt as if God was sustaining me by the power of His presence!

We heard gunshots ring out on a neighboring yard that day, and everyone had to get down on the ground. However, there were no shots fired on C yard that entire day! By the end of the afternoon session, I looked around and reflected on God's grace and protection. We had not seen any violence on C yard all day.

I was sharing this with an inmate. He looked at me and said, "Do you really want to know what happened?" I said, "yes," and he then explained, "Look around, don't you see these gangs? They are highly organized and run this yard. Within the gangs are generals, shot callers, foot soldiers, and associates. Yesterday, the generals of these gangs found out you guys were coming out onto the yard today, and therefore they got word to one another and called a truce, just for the day."

I could not believe what I was hearing. God had moved on the generals of the most violent gangs, in likely the most violent prison yard in America, to call a truce so we could be protected to proclaim His Word!!!

*God is faithful.*

In November of 2012, the Lord gave me an open door to go to the country of Nigeria. I had never been out of the United States before and traveled to a huge city called Lagos. It is the biggest city in Africa in terms of population, having about 15 million people. It was a tremendous growth experience for me.

I have never experienced so much spiritual warfare before, nor have I been given so many blessings in such a short amount of time. I was gone for about seven days. I got there on a Friday and on Sunday the Lord opened an opportunity for me to speak to around 3,000

Nigerians at a worship service. I was there for about four and a half hours and never had seen such earnest worship for such a long period of time.

There was dancing and praising and dedications for babies and so much prayer. The intensity of the prayer, the number of worshipers, and the joyous dancing was simply awe-inspiring. There were five offerings in that single service. And not only were they offerings, but the people would dance all the way up to the front of the congregation and drop off their offerings into a large basket. It was incredible.

What an honor it was to be able to speak to and encourage them. I was there with a team of volunteers for a short period of time to distribute a lot of Bibles in the cities of Lagos and Ibadan. The next day, Monday, we gave away about 150,000 copies of the Word of God. The day after, Tuesday, we gave away another 125,000. So, within a forty-eight-hour period, 275,000 copies had gone out, and the Lord was giving us open door after open door after open door.

My first ten minutes on the ground Monday morning just blew me away. I found myself at a primary school, and the headmaster there welcomed us as we pulled in. We were running late, and he said, "You have five minutes to address these children." They had the kids pulled out from all the different buildings of the school to the middle of the courtyard, which was an open field. Just to get to address them was so humbling. With all eyes on me, the hundreds of kids looked up in awe to see someone that had light skin.

There were 651 kids in that courtyard that morning. I got to give them the Good News of God's love. After sharing the Gospel, I shared that if they would like to, just between them and God, they could pray to receive Jesus as their Savior.

As we said that prayer together, the presence of God was so strong that my voice began to crack, and I barely got through that prayer. The tears began to stream down my face. We gave out those 651 Scriptures to each one of those kids that morning. The kids would come up and actually bow to receive God's Word—with thankfulness and respect. It was amazing.

The next day we found ourselves in a parking area for a school with which we had no relationship. We looked at the sign of the school and realized it was a Muslim school. Sitting in the car, we prayed for an open door. We literally just showed up without an invitation or any kind of a relationship with this school. There were just four of us sitting in a car with a thousand Bibles in the trunk. What can you do? So, we just started praying, asking God to open the door.

When the locals asked permission, the Muslim headmaster allowed us to come in to give Bibles to the kids. Not only did he allow us to do so, but we got to speak to them. He pulled them out of all their buildings and brought them to middle courtyard like what happened the day before. We were able to share with them the Gospel, and when asked if they wanted to receive Jesus, dozens of hands went up to say, "yes." It was one of those amazing experiences that could only be from God.

It was so humbling to go to school after school after school. In many, we went inside of the classrooms and were able to give copies of God's Word to the students as they were sitting at their desks. They were so happy, and their eyes were so bright.

Those eyes...I could never express in words the glow in their eyes and how thankful they were that we were there. It made them feel so special that someone would come from such a far land to tell them that God loves them, and to give them copies of His Word. In some cases, it might have been the only new book that they would ever see for years, or even possibly for a good portion of their lifetime. There were many, many instances of seeing God's grace move repeatedly and how evident and important it was for these people to hear the Good News of the Gospel, and to receive a copy of God's Word.

What an amazing experience by the grace of God to have that opportunity to see just how God would go before us and move on hearts; even on those that might not even have a relationship with Him. I think of that Muslim headmaster. I have a photo of him standing there, looking at me as I am praying with his students for them to receive Jesus.

That is a moment I hope to never forget. God's grace is amazing, and He is so faithful. By the end of the two-week period, the rest of the team had given out about 703,000 copies of the Word of God, to the glory of God!

After a long day during a mission trip in New York City, I returned to my hotel in Queens. To save money on travel costs, the volunteers on the trip split the hotel costs by sharing rooms with two beds. I entered the room and my roommate was watching television. He was trying to watch a football game, but the station was not working.

He called the hotel receptionist, and she told him they would send someone up. Before long, there was a knock at the door. Unaware of the request, I opened the door and saw the hotel employee. He shared that he was a maintenance man to check on the television.

I invited him in and began a conversation as he worked on the television. I found out that he was from the Dominican Republic. Frustrated, he could not get the channel to work. We encouraged him and then began to share the Gospel.

I gave him a Bible in his native language of Spanish, and he graciously accepted it. After offering him an invitation to receive Christ, he accepted, and we all bowed our heads as he received Christ! Just then, the television channel started working, and he left the room. It was as if God stopped the channel from working to orchestrate a divine appointment!

After several months of entering a solitary confinement unit of the maximum-security prison in the state where I live, I began to develop good relationships with the inmates as I interacted with them through the steel doors. On occasion, the doors had their pie flaps open, so I could kneel and talk with the men face to face.

God was blessing the efforts as the inmates were willing to talk about the Bible and receive prayer. I was greatly surprised one day when an inmate shared the following. He said, "Look around the unit. There is peace. That is unusual. It's as if when you enter in here, the demons flee." I was stunned by his description of sensing the environment in such a directly spiritual way.

*God honors His Word, even amid an oppressed environment.*

# Chapter 12

## *Believe and Follow*

As I continued to learn to simply believe and follow the Lord, throughout the journey, He would continue to allow me to be a part of His redemptive work in the lives of others. In Matthew 4:19, we read:

> "And he said to them, 'Follow me, and I will make you fishers of men.'"

One day after lunch, I took some time to reflect and pray. It was during this time, I felt the Lord speak to me, again in that still small voice. He said, "I want you to blanket the prison with my Word." I was stunned and a bit overwhelmed by what I heard. I was not sure how it would come about, but I knew that if the Lord was directing, He would make a way for it to happen.

I immediately called another prison volunteer and told him what the Lord said to me. He responded that he would be willing to meet me at the prison later in the day. Late that afternoon, we arrived at the prison parking lot with hundreds of Bibles and a metal handcart. We prayed and then began to truck the Bibles into the lobby of the security intake building.

I prayed fervently that the Lord would give us the words to say. We had not called the prison in advance to request permission for this Bible distribution to occur. As we walked into the lobby, the officers looked at us from their desks. There was an awkward silence, and as I prayed for the words to say, the Lord prompted me to not say anything. Therefore, I remained silent as we approached the security checkpoint.

Finally, an officer spoke up and asked what we had. I told him we had Bibles for all the inmates. After another pause, he said, "Okay, send them through the scanner." We began to unbox and send all the hundreds of Bibles through the scanner. This took some time, and a line of officers began to form behind us as they were waiting to go through security to enter the prison for their shifts. As the tension rose, I realized the spiritual battle that was occurring, but the Lord prompted me to remain quiet and trust in Him.

After all the Bibles were sent though the scanner, we had to walk through a metal detector. We had to roll the metal handcart through the detector as well. The scanner began to alarm, but the officer waived us though. Then, a large steel door was opened, and we began to truck the hundreds of Bibles freely throughout the maximum-security prison, hand-delivering the Bibles to inmates, cell by cell, unit by unit, building by building.

We were truly stunned and astonished, but also reminded of the sovereignty of God and how He was honoring His Word. God was pursuing the lives of the men in the prison, and what a joy it was for us to follow the Lord as fishers of men!

Years ago, I was on a ministry assignment in Los Angeles, CA. One day I had to travel from the west side of town to the east side. Traffic was horrific, and it literally took me about three and a half hours to travel around thirty miles. As I was stuck on an interstate with standstill traffic, I decided to look on a map to see if there was another route. I noticed another interstate going parallel from west to east, but it was a bit north from where I was.

At the appropriate time, I exited off the interstate with standstill traffic and began to cut north to try and get to the other interstate. As I was heading northbound, I drove up near downtown Los Angeles on the west side. I approached and passed by a large park, called MacArthur Park. As I drove by, I could not believe what I saw.

There was so much poverty and homelessness. Among the crowds of people, I saw so many things. There were people pushing carts with their belongings, and many other people with items laid out on blankets as they tried to sell things to people passing by. I also saw a truck parked near a sidewalk offering free HIV screenings. I was shocked at the level of poverty. I thought that God did not bring me there by accident, so I started to pray. I began to fervently intercede for the people and kept driving.

I eventually found my way to the northern interstate and went on my way. However, I could not get the vision of the people I saw out of my mind. I felt a burden for them and continued to pray. A thought and question came to my mind, "Lord, are you calling me to go there and share the Gospel?" I told the Lord I would be faithful to do what He wanted. I finished my assignment there and flew back home.

A few weeks went by and I continued to pray. I had it on my calendar to travel back to Los Angeles again. I told the Lord if He would supply His Word, I would be faithful to give it out. One day I was in the mail room of my office and I reached up to get a box off the shelf. The box flipped over, and the contents spilled out toward the floor over my head. To my surprise, they were Spanish language Bibles!

It was as if God was literally raining His Word down on me. I immediately recalled the multitude of Hispanic people and businesses I had seen in and around MacArthur Park in Los Angeles and said, "Ok God, I get it."

I packed a suitcase full of those Spanish Bibles and got ready for my trip. The day I was scheduled to leave, I felt the Lord wake me up early in the morning and prompted me to pray. I began to think of the people at MacArthur Park and continued to pray for them.

The Lord gave me more of a burden for them, and then a thought came to me, "Who am I that the Lord would allow me to bring His Word to these people?" I began to weep. I cried harder than I had in years. I felt so humbled and honored. I asked God to lead the way and to prepare hearts to receive His Word.

That day, I went to the airport and loaded my suitcases on the ticketing gate counter. To my surprise, the luggage with the Bibles weighed forty-eight pounds, just under the fifty-pound limit! As the attendant took the heavy bag and put a tag on it, I praised God for His provision. I flew to Los Angeles in anticipation of what God wanted to do.

While I was there, I was blessed to speak at several events encouraging others to be on mission for God. At the first event, I was in Santa Monica and at the second event, I was in Orange County in a city called Fullerton. At the second event after I spoke, I went to mingle with people in the crowd. I happened to tell one man in attendance that I was planning to go to MacArthur Park to share the Gospel. His immediate response was "Do you have a gun?" I replied, "no," and then he told me how dangerous it was there. He said, "Even the police don't go there!"

At the time, MacArthur Park was a notorious area for drugs and gang-related activity. Another man in attendance at the event, named Pablo, asked me if I spoke Spanish, and I told him, "no." He then shared that he was from Santa Monica and missed the first event, so he had driven down to be at the second event. Pablo also shared that he spoke Spanish. I invited him if he wanted to come with me, but he said he had to work the following day. I asked him to pray for me, and he said he would.

The next morning, I woke up in eager anticipation as I had been praying about this day for weeks. Suddenly, I began to experience very negative thoughts and visions. I heard a voice say "You don't know what you are doing. You don't belong here. You will be hurt." I then saw an imaginary vision of me getting shot in the stomach at MacArthur Park and dying a slow and painful death. It was horrible, so I fell on the floor in the hotel and began to pray.

As I sought the Lord, I confessed that I was lost without Him, and remembered all the times the Lord brought me to prayer about MacArthur Park. I could not understand why He would bring me all this way and then close the door. I asked Him for clarity on what to do. At that moment in deep prayer, I heard the Lord clearly say "Go. Go now."

I jumped up off the floor with a renewed vision for God's calling. It felt as if the Holy Spirit was pouring over me, and I had a supernatural confidence. Then God whispered for me to call Pablo.

I called him to let him know I was going. He answered by saying, "You won't believe this, but my schedule just completely freed up. I can meet you there." I said "Great!" I drove north as he drove east, and we met downtown at MacArthur Park. After a time of prayer, we began walking into the park as I wheeled my suitcase full of Bibles behind me.

God began to open doors to share Christ with others. I was amazed at the receptivity as we began to offer people Bibles and prayer. Then, an interesting thing happened. About the third person we had a conversation with was a man who only spoke Spanish. Pablo began to talk with him as I stood by.

I was looking around as they engaged in conversation. Then, the Lord prompted me that we needed to ask the man if he was saved. I interrupted their conversation to share what the Lord had put on my heart with Pablo. He responded that that was exactly what they were talking about. I kept praying, and a few moments later we were laying hands on the man, praying with him to receive Jesus!

The man and Pablo exchanged a few more words and then we were on our way. God blessed us tremendously that day. Over the next few hours, we witnessed to and gave away Bibles to hundreds of people. God had His hand of protection on us and there were no violent encounters with hostile people. Afterward, we were hungry, so we went to a local spot to eat. It was a run-down building that served chicken. As we were eating lunch, Pablo and I shared in excitement what we had just experienced.

I said, "Hey Pablo, that was awesome! Remember the third guy we met earlier?" He said, "Yes, the man's name was Hector." I clearly remembered that moment being a special move of God, and I said, "Yes him. I remember you and he said a few things after our prayer with him. What did he say?"

Pablo looked at me with an excited expression and said, "Do you really want to know what he said?" I said, "yes," and Pablo said, "He told me he woke up that morning, looked up to the sky and said, 'God, if you show me how, I will give my life to you.'" There we were just a few hours later, standing in front of Hector, sharing the Gospel with him, and watching him give his life to the Lord. Hallelujah!

*God had blessed me tremendously as I followed Him.*

God even provided a translator at the last minute to ensure His Word was proclaimed. Sometimes, as we follow the Lord, we have no clue of what the result will be. It seems He wants us to follow Him through the journey.

On a trip to New York City, God put it on my heart to load up a van full of Bibles to distribute at homeless shelters in Manhattan. I loaded up the van and took another volunteer named Vernon with me. As we began to cross the bridge into the city, we could strongly sense God's presence. We both knew God was with us. After crossing into Manhattan, we drove a few blocks as we prayed for God to lead us. To our surprise, we located a homeless shelter, and there were over a hundred people stretched down the block. We parked the van and realized it was a feeding line. We carried boxes of Bibles to the front of the line where the food tables were.

After people went through the line, we began to offer them Bibles. Many took the Bibles and then we started having conversations. God opened opportunities to share the Gospel and offer prayer. Many individuals received prayer support for a variety of issues and concerns.

I remember there was a young couple who were very receptive. After sharing the Good News, both responded by praying to receive Jesus as their Savior. God had directed our paths right where we needed to be, even amid a tremendously busy city. What a blessing!

*It is amazing what happens as we simply believe and follow Him.*

*Grace Upon Grace*

# Chapter 13

## Sufficient Grace Through Trials

Throughout this book, I have shared many highlights of great experiences. As I shared earlier, things may not always be easy, but God has a way of drawing us closer to Him even through times of trials. In 2 Corinthians 12:9, we read:

> "But he said to me, 'My grace is sufficient for you, for my power is made perfect in weakness.' Therefore I will boast all the more gladly of my weaknesses, so that the power of Christ may rest upon me."

Also, in Luke 9:23, we read:

> "And he said to all, 'If anyone would come after me, let him deny himself and take up his cross daily and follow me.'"

Throughout the Christian journey, there will inevitably be times of trials. Sometimes, we do not understand why these trials occur as we follow the Lord, but they do. We can learn from them, but most importantly can draw closer to God through them.

On my mission trip to Nigeria, I experienced a trial that was completely unexpected. On my second day there, I began to experience insomnia and anxiety at a heightened level. I prayed through the night and God drew me closer to Him through His Word. He directed me to the following Scripture verse from Psalm 37:3, which literally felt like it jumped off the page.

> "Trust in the Lord, and do good;
> Dwell in the land, and feed on His faithfulness."

I was encouraged, and the next day was blessed to speak at a large church in front of 3,000 people. However, that evening I experienced more insomnia and anxiety, and unexpectedly began to see and hear things that were not there. Surprisingly, I began to experience hallucinations.

After the third evening of sleep deprivation, I continued the work of the mission and shared the Gospel with hundreds of students. That evening, I experienced more sleeplessness and hallucinations. Not understanding what was happening, I thought I was under a severe spiritual attack. I read Scripture over and over and committed it to prayer. The fourth evening, the same thing occurred.

By the fifth day, my body began to react to the fatigue as well as hypertension resulting from the stress of the hallucinations. I felt moments of adrenaline followed by a sense of exhaustion. My heartbeat became irregular and I worried what would happen. I ended up catching a flight back home that evening, experiencing ongoing anxiety, a continued lack of appetite, and sleep deprivation for a fifth day in a row.

Upon my return to my hometown, still unable to sleep, I went to a local hospital for examination by a doctor. It was determined that I was experiencing a reaction to the malaria medication that I had begun taking at the start of the trip. Why did this happen? Why would the Lord take me halfway around the world to experience such a trial?

Although the answers to these questions may yet remain fully unknown to me, I can rest in God's promise from Romans 8:28, that He is working all things for my good. Maybe He was protecting me from something worse, or maybe it was simply a trial to learn more of His sufficient grace through suffering. Even through the trial, I was still used of God to serve in Nigeria and praise Him for the blessing.

I can remember another journey the Lord took me on that captures an experience of unusual trials. I was invited to give a presentation on evangelism in a small town in central North Dakota. I planned the trip in conjunction with another prior one where I had traveled to southern California. I departed from Los

Angeles International Airport and had a layover in Minneapolis, Minnesota before heading to Jamestown, North Dakota.

The weather in southern California was warm and I was wearing a short-sleeved shirt. I had a jacket with me in preparation for my trip to North Dakota but decided not to bring it with me on the airplane and instead packed it in my luggage. When I arrived in Minneapolis, I was surprised to see a snowstorm outside.

I proceeded to the gate to get a boarding pass for the flight to North Dakota. To my surprise, the boarding slip looked more like a receipt than a normal boarding pass. I then asked the attendant at the counter if I could request a window seat. She replied that I did have a window seat. I was thankful and headed off to the boarding gate.

When I arrived at the terminal, I looked out the window and saw the snow. To my surprise, I also saw the plane in the distance. It was so small that apparently the commercial airline I bought my flight through had subcontracted that portion of the trip to a smaller airline carrier. In fact, the plane was so small it was sitting off in the distance on the tarmac.

I immediately realized I would have to walk outside in my short sleeve shirt to get on the plane. As I hurried to the plane with my carry-on bag which did not have my jacket in it, the baggage attendant looked at me as I approached the plane through his snow goggles, wearing a heavy outfit with gloves. I thought it was a funny moment as I hurriedly entered the plane.

As I stepped into the plane, I saw what the flight attendant meant by me having a window seat. The plane only had a few seats and they were all window seats! I gripped my seat as the pilots fired up the propellers. The wind blew heavily as we took off, and it appeared the windows were freezing up so that it was hard to see out of them.

I looked up front. Since the plane was so small, the pilots did not have a door to the cockpit, and I could see them. Then I noticed they also had limited visibility. I could feel the plane being tossed around by the wind through the snow. I could barely see a multitude of small lakes on the ground below out of the window. I began to pray.

After touching down an hour or so later in Jamestown, I praised God for His protection. I entered the small regional airport as the sun was setting. I looked for the car rental counter. There was a small sign for the car rental company hanging by two chains, but the desk was empty.

An airport attendant shared that the rental car person left hours ago. They then went to turn the airport lobby lights off. I asked if there was a local taxicab company to take me to my hotel and there was only one in town. I called the number and a cab came to get me.

As the cab driver approached the airport, he parked and opened the trunk. I placed my luggage in the trunk, but the trunk would not close. I slammed it a few times before it latched shut. The driver then told me to sit in the front seat. I was surprised to see that he was not wearing a shirt, and had white bandages wrapped around his torso. As he drove me to the hotel, he explained that he had just gotten out of the hospital. I checked into the hotel and was glad to finally rest.

The next day, I conducted the evangelism training, had some lunch, and then went back to the hotel. Early that evening I began to get severely sick. I started to vomit uncontrollably. This went on for hours. I continued to dry-heave as my body was clearly reacting to something. Hours later, I finally called the local hospital. I checked into the emergency room and was told there was a 24-hour bug going around town. I remembered the cab driver and wondered if he had passed it to me.

So, there I was, in a hospital bed in central North Dakota, attached to a bag of saline solution that was intravenously being injected into my body to rehydrate and strengthen me. After a few hours in the hospital and after a second bag of the solution had depleted, the doctor released me with some prescription medication. It took several days to recover before I could travel back home. What a trip and set of trials through which to trust God.

*He is faithful!*

Another time I found myself in quite a precarious situation. I was in Rikers Island, the world's largest jail. A few volunteers and I were in a chapel waiting for inmates to arrive for a church service. As I prayed, I realized I needed to use the restroom. I asked an officer if this was possible, and she gave me a set of keys and told me where to go.

I walked down a hall and found the restroom. I opened the locked door with the keys and used the facility. Then, to my surprise as I tried to exit, the door would not open. No matter how many times I shook the handle it would not open. Somehow the door was configured so that it would not open from the inside with the doorknob. After several minutes, I realized I was simply locked in.

This was not a good feeling. Imagine being locked inside a small bathroom in the world's largest jail. I tried not to get anxious as reality set in. I banged on the door for minutes on end, but nobody responded. I continued to try to open the door, but it would not. I began to pace and pray, beginning to give up and wondering what would happen. How long would I have to be stuck in this place?

I prayed more and asked God for peace and discernment during this uneasy challenge. I knew the chapel was far down the hall and it could be some time before an officer found me. I walked back to the door. The lock was in the open position and the knob would still not be effective in opening the door.

Against my own intuition, I decided to try and lock the door. As I put the lock in the forward position, it moved even further and to my great surprise the door opened. I could not believe it! I walked back to the chapel and God gave us a great service. I was even blessed to lead many inmates to the Lord during that service.

*God's grace is sufficient!*

# Chapter 14

## Helping Others

It has become increasingly evident that God blesses the efforts of helping others grow in their faith through their service unto Him. In Hebrews 6:10, we read:

> "For God is not unjust so as to overlook your work and the love that you have shown for his name in serving the saints, as you still do."

I believe that God does not always want us to experience His blessings alone. One such case comes to mind. I was on a bus in Dallas, Texas going out to the streets to share the Gospel. There was a couple near me on the bus from northern California. They shared with me that they were not used to street ministry and wanted to tag along. This is quite normal as most people feel apprehensive initially to share their faith. I agreed to their request.

The man's name was Bob, and his wife's name was Shelley. Bob served as the missions' chairman for his church for twenty-five years. He helped support and commission missionaries all over the world but was not used to sharing Christ with people on the streets. Shelley mentioned to me that she was nervous and did not know what to say to people, either. I told them that it was not about us, but what God wanted to do through us. Our job was to pray, and so we did.

The bus stopped and we got off near a crowded Dallas Area Rapid Transit train station. There were many people walking around. God led me to start talking to a Hispanic man. Bob and Shelley were standing nearby. As God opened the door, I shared the Gospel with the man. Conviction fell upon him, and he started to weep heavily. He prayed earnestly to receive Christ as his tears fell on the sidewalk.

Bob and Shelley were stunned as they watched what was happening. Just then, another lady came walking up to us, and without us even saying a word to her, she proclaimed, "I need to be saved." Stunned, I looked over at Shelley and said, "Are you ready?" Shelley said, "yes," and then began to share the Gospel with the lady. Afterward, Shelley had the blessing of leading this lady to Christ.

Shelley's whole demeanor changed as she realized it was not about her, but rather it was about watching God draw others to Himself. She realized her job was to trust wholly in the Lord, and so she began sharing Christ with so many people that day. It was marvelous. The last I heard, Shelley had since started her own street ministry in Sacramento, California, and her husband Bob went on to become a volunteer chaplain at Folsom State Prison.

*Praise God for the opportunities He gives us to invest in the lives of others, so they can continue to grow in their confidence in the Lord and bear fruit for years to come.*

Another opportunity where I saw this play out was in St. Augustine, Florida. I had conducted an evangelism training for a small group and then encouraged everyone to pray. Everyone got on their knees and began to vocalize fervent prayer. The second-to-the-last person to pray was especially moving to me. The man prayed openly and honestly before God, asking Him to help him. He confessed that he was not used to sharing the Gospel with others and needed to depend fully on the Lord.

After the prayer time, I approached the man, named Byron. I asked if he wanted to go along with me, and he agreed. We drove to the historical downtown area near St. George Street and parked the car. We prayed and then started walking the heavily touristed area looking for opportunities to talk to people about the Lord. God opened many doors to give people a copy of His Word and tell them about Jesus.

Byron watched as one homeless woman prayed to receive Christ on the sidewalk. We got down to our last two Bibles as we walked down the street. I asked Byron if God opened a door, would he like to pray with someone to receive Christ. He said, "yes."

It was about that time, I looked down the long road full of people walking around and, in the distance, I saw an old Spanish fort. Since I had never been to St. Augustine before, I asked Byron if we could take a closer look. He agreed and off we went.

As we approached the large fort, we were walking down a sidewalk. The Lord prompted me to stop and speak to a couple sitting on a nearby park bench. This was an older couple from India. We began to speak with them, and then offered our last two Bibles to them. They graciously accepted the Bibles, and then we began to share the Good News. The couple wanted to pray, so I again asked Byron if he was ready. Byron then kneeled next to the couple and began to pray with them to receive Christ.

During the prayer, I became convicted that the lady was not fully understanding. She shared that she was having a hard time understanding as English was not her native language. At that very moment, her daughter came walking up. She told us to speak with her daughter who would then translate for her in her native language. We then shared the Gospel with her daughter so she could translate. Before we knew it, we were praying with the whole family to receive Christ!

As we walked away, we could sense the presence of God. Byron got on-fire to start telling others about Jesus, as he realized it was not about him, but rather what God could do through him. Hallelujah!

It is truly humbling that God allows us to be a part of His eternally significant redemptive work in the lives of others; all by His grace and for His glory. As we conclude, let us reflect upon God's Word. We read in 2 Corinthians 5:

"[16] From now on, therefore, we regard no one according to the flesh. Even though we once regarded Christ according to the flesh, we regard him thus no longer. [17] Therefore, if anyone is in Christ, he is a new creation. The old has passed away; behold, the new has come. [18] All this is from God, who through Christ reconciled us to himself and gave us the ministry of reconciliation; [19] that is, in Christ God was reconciling the world to himself, not counting their trespasses against them, and entrusting to us the message of reconciliation. [20] Therefore, we are ambassadors for Christ, God making his appeal through us. We implore you on behalf of Christ, be reconciled to God. [21] For our sake he made him to be sin who knew no sin, so that in him we might become the righteousness of God."

*To God alone be all praise, honor, and glory!*

# Epilogue

Now that you have read through these testimonies of God's grace as He draws us closer to Himself, I'd like to encourage you to take some time to reflect on what this might mean for you. As we have seen, God does not force Himself on anyone, but He pursues each of us through His amazing love.

*Have you experienced the love of God in Christ?*

*Is God pursuing you even at this very moment?*

It is your choice to unlock the door to your heart and allow in Jesus Christ. The very same truths that are permeating throughout the book are available to you at this very moment.

Let us be very clear. God loves you. He gave His Son, Jesus, to die on a cross for you. He can forgive you of your sins. You can receive the gift of eternal life. You can open your heart and pray now:

God, I am ready to open my heart to you.

I do now confess and receive

Jesus as my Lord and Savior.

Please save me.

Please forgive me.

I surrender my life to You.

In Jesus' name. Amen.

Made in the USA
Las Vegas, NV
21 November 2022

59971335R00097